This (Book) Is Dedicated to

the One(s) I Love

To Joe, Tracy, Brian, and Chuck

Get your motor running.

Head out on the highway,

Looking for adventure,

For whatever comes our way.

To Carol

Yeah, darling, gonna make it happen.

CONTENTS

PREFACE

Jay Leno called.

He was gracious enough to rewrite one of the jokes as well as give me some ideas. He suggested the title be changed. I thought the title *Don't Eat the Yellow Snow and Everything Else a Graduating Senior Should Know* was pretty good. Jay thought it should be more original.

I don't respect many people, but Leno is one of my heroes. I usually follow what my gut tells me, but when someone I admire gives me advice, I try to take it.

I spent the next three days coming up with more titles:

> Being a Student Isn't So Bad When You Find You Can't Get a Job
>
> What I Needed to Know Once I Had Learned Everything
>
> Treat your Body As If It's the Only One You'll Ever Have
>
> How to Take the Golden Rule Platinum

My students know the answer to every marketing problem lies with the customer. Who is the customer for this book? Students. Duuuuh. All I had to do was ask my students for ideas. Here are some of the two hundred titles they submitted:

> Why Didn't My Professors Tell Me That?
>
> A Student's Guide to Life After College (or How to Survive in the Real World)
>
> A Graduating Senior's Survival Guide: What They Didn't Teach You in College
>
> Everything College Was Supposed to Prepare You For, but Didn't
>
> Real Life 101
>
> All the Important Stuff Your College Profs Forgot to Teach You
>
> What a College Senior Should Know When the Barrel Is Empty and the Party Is Over
>
> Graduating Seniors: What the Textbooks Didn't Teach You but Should Have

I then took the students' submissions and my best ideas, including the original title, and surveyed all my students (they didn't know which titles were mine).

The results:

First place	What a College Senior Should Know When the Barrel Is Empty and the Party Is Over
Second place	A Graduating Senior's Survival Guide: What They Didn't Teach You in College
Third place	Real Life 101
Fourth place	All the Important Stuff Your College Profs Forgot to Teach You

You'll note none of mine placed. Not much satisfaction for my ego.

I then published the book myself, using the winning title.

Although I loved the title my students had created, when Simon & Schuster decided to publish my book, they thought the book had a broader appeal than just to college seniors. The new title, *Life etc.: Advice for the Real World,* is the result of the Simon & Schuster brains trust. (I trust their brains.) I knew Simon & Schuster was right. When I wrote it I thought the market was going to be college seniors, but I soon found out over 90 percent of those who bought it were over forty, to give as a gift to their children or grandchildren for both pre- and post-graduation.

Thanks, students.
Thanks, Jay Leno.
Thanks, Bill Trumbull and Chris Core.
Thanks, David Kroll.
Thanks, Carolyn Reidy.
Thanks, Betsy Radin.

INTRODUCTION

Don't worry about being young. You'll outgrow it.

At the end of each semester I play "Viewer Mail" with my students. I pass out 3 x 5 cards and tell them to ask any question they wish . . . and they don't have to put their names on the cards.

I explain if I know the answer, I will answer the question. But if I don't know the answer, I'll *still* answer the question. This book contains my responses to all those questions my thousands of college students have asked me over the last decade. These responses represent my beliefs, the things I have learned in business and in life.

I hope I don't come off as a know-it-all. I'm not, because I don't. Most of what I believe is the result of some very costly errors. I may not know what to do all the time, but I do know many things not to do—because I've done them. Sometimes, just to make sure I was wrong, I'd make the same mistake twice.

Experience is the name everyone gives to our mistakes.

I realize some who read this will think of me as an

idealist. Everyone's idealism increases the farther away they are from the problem. Others will think I have little tolerance. And the thought police of the academic community have labeled me as a politically incorrect full mooner.

The older I get, the less I know.

Perhaps.

If your mind enjoys the challenge of a Beavis jump cut, this might be for you. Tidbits come out in Uzi fashion, splattering all over the place, but now and then I try to let the barrel cool with a personal experience.

However, if you are looking for a thematic focus, you should stop reading now. Students ask shotgun questions ("How do I get promoted fast?" "What do I need to do to start my own business?" "Why believe in God?"), and answers defy any point of convergence. Specific questions can have detailed answers, but generic questions must be answered in a generalized way.

And if you are over thirty, you probably think, "Hey, everyone knows this." Some do, but many don't.

When I finished the first draft, I thought it would be interesting to see which of the thoughts I'd written were something I'd created. I did some research. Bad news for me. There doesn't seem to be much original. I started to think nothing I could say was something that hadn't been said before. Even the last sentence was something the playwright Terence said in 160 B.C. His words were exactly "mine," or should I say my words were exactly "his"? As I did the research, I did find a few new quotes that summarized what I was trying to say, and I added these as I found them. So, for those who are interested, I have included in the appendixes sources of those who said what I have said.

A lot of what you will read are my opinions. This is the way I feel today. Some thoughts have changed since I was young, but some are exactly the same—or at least the basics were there and have become more crystallized over the years. Some may change in the future, but I doubt it.

If you always do what you've always done, you'll always get what you've always got. That's not bad if you are always doing the right thing. When I first started off in business, I thought the right thing was what I had learned in the classroom. It took me some time to find out the right thing was what I learned from my parents and from my life. What is simple is seldom understood.

Life was half over before I knew what life was. But, when you're over the hill, you begin to pick up speed. Hopefully this book will allow some students entering the work world to fast-forward past those street learning years I had to go through. It might

This book contains what I needed to know once I had learned everything.

mean kissing fewer frogs before finding a Prince Charming.

When I started this book, I thought the finished product would be something profound, something great. Now that it is done, I'm not so sure. I'm honored that you will spend your time and money on this book. Whether it is of value is for you to judge.

I've always found it good to know the baggage the speaker is carrying so I can understand why he or she says what they say. The rest of this chapter is about me, so you can better judge the rest of the book. But, if you're like me, sometimes you want to get to the meat first to find out if something is worth the time.

If you're looking for some pages to skip, the next five would be the ones.

My father was a career naval officer. We moved every three or four years. It is a great way to be brought up. My mother was from a family that lost everything during the Depression, but she still maintained her political contacts. Mom and Robert Kennedy used to dance professionally together when they were young.

I wanted to go to the Naval Academy, as my dad had, but I was too young when I graduated from high school to be admitted. I went to Virginia Tech instead.

I met Carol when we were both very young, and

we married young. Our first son was born while I was at Tech. I graduated with degrees in mechanical engineering and business administration, then taught mathematics at Radford College and industrial engineering at Virginia Tech.

My first job in the real world was as an industrial engineer with Kodak. That didn't last long. I was a captain in the army from 1967 to 1970. During that time, another son and a daughter were born. While I was in the army, I also got my MBA and published my first book on the stock market.

After the service, I went to work for a Fortune 500 company located in La Crosse, Wisconsin. My wife loved the town, and I loved the work. My job was starting up businesses, dismantling businesses that weren't doing well, and preparing acquisitions. A great learning opportunity. I would have been willing to pay them to work there. After I had been there about three years, I walked in one day and found out I was fired.

On the way home to see Carol I was trying to figure out how I would tell her. Although we had just about paid off all my college loans, we had about $600 in the bank, no real assets, and three children. When I got home, I told her I had some great news—I had been fired. Naturally, she was wondering why this was so wonderful. I told her she could decide where in the world we would live. We would auction off everything, put the kids in the car, go there, and settle down. I convinced her a chance like this will only happen a very few times in our lifetime.

Carol is cosmopolitan. Her daddy was an FBI agent. This meant she had seen a lot of places growing up, and since part of our duty in the army had been spent in Europe, for a young person, Carol really understood the world fairly well.

A week later she told me she had made her decision. She wanted to stay in La Crosse.

Your whole life comes down to a few decision points. I knew this was going to be one of mine. I gritted my teeth, managed a broken smile, and said, "Great!"

La Crosse is a beautiful town. Compared to most cities in the United States, it has little crime and little pollution. A perfect spot to live. But when I was fired, my impression of La Crosse was that it was nothing but a bunch of houses. My job for the Fortune 500 company required me to be on a plane from Monday through Friday. I spent so much time flying, I wrote my second book—on entrepreneurship—entirely on planes.

I traveled so much my own dog would bite me.

I had no idea what industry was in the town. After spending a day looking through the yellow pages and talking with the people at the Chamber of Commerce, I came to the conclusion that if I wanted to stay in La Crosse, I was going to have to start up a business of my own.

All business students know the best kind of business to have is a monopoly. Why? So you can control prices. I made a list of everything I had seen all around the world but that had not yet made it to La Crosse. At that time there wasn't a self-pump gas station, an automatic car wash, a condominium, indoor tennis courts, etc., etc. Then I tried to do a market and profit analysis on each.

It came down to condominiums or indoor tennis courts. I had never been in a condominium, and I had played tennis about five times in my life. But, you don't have to be a wizard to figure out which would be more fun. Sure. Run around in your shorts and make money. I was going into the indoor tennis court business.

I sat down. Typed out a prospectus. I made myself the general partner and decided to sell limited partnership units. I had a friend who was a member of the country club. I asked him to get me a membership list. Then I asked him who loved tennis and had lots of money. I started knocking on doors—I had never met any of the potential investors before then. In short order I had $200,000. I then went to the bank, actually several banks, and got a loan for another $400,000. The construction of the club began.

Murphy's law held. Construction delays. Cost overruns. Arguments with the investors and contractors. But, finally, it was open.

The first five years were terrible. I was on the verge of bankruptcy all the time. Finally, I decided the only way the business was going to make it was to either turn the place into a warehouse or diversify into other forms of recreation. I wasn't thrilled with the thought of storing beer for a living, so I decided to add racquetball.

Some of my investors were very supportive during the bad years—they would put more money in when I'd get to a $50,000 negative balance in my checking account. But even for the best partners, the racquetball was the last straw. They all said no.

I said, no problem. I went ahead and started another partnership. This one was for racquetball. That partnership leased space from the tennis partnership. No conflict. It was structured so the tennis partnership always got a good deal. I went out, raised another $200,000, and built the racquetball courts.

Then an amazing thing happened. The club started breaking even.

A small fitness center opened nearby. I saw some of my members leaving my club and joining the fitness center. I went over and looked at the equipment. I had no idea what it was, but I could see my members joining that club. I called the supplier of the equipment and told him I would take exactly what he had sold to my competitor. Exactly the same. I did have to get another $60,000 loan from a local bank to buy the exercise equipment. Not only was I in the tennis and racquetball business, I was now in the fitness business.

Then an even more astounding thing happened. The club actually started making money. And as there was profit, I could then afford to improve the club, add a big aerobics room, a gigantic exercise equipment area, a cardiovascular center, swimming pool, whirlpool, babysitting, physical therapy, karate, and on and on. Today, at least at the time of publication, the club makes money.

As my business became profitable, I no longer had to put in eighty hours a week—in fact, a lot less. One day I got a call from the University of Wisconsin in La Crosse. The semester had just started and one of their finance professors had quit. They asked me if I would be willing to teach the class. Sure! Ten years later, I'm still teaching and have been in the marketing department for several years.

I consider teaching an enjoyable mental break in the day.

A visiting friend went to our local newsstand and asked for a copy of *USA Today.*

"Would you like yesterday's issue or today's?"

"Today's, of course."

"Well, then, come back tomorrow."

1 ATTITUDE

If you think you can or you can't, you're right.

WITHIN THE PRISON WALLS OF MY MIND

Aptitude is what you could become. Attitude is what you do become.

Your attitude determines just what kind of life you will have. You will have a great time living if you think you will.

You are what you think you are, and you become what you think you will become.

CRIMSON AND CLOVER OVER AND OVER

Who do you think controls your attitude? You do. If you control what you think and you become what you believe you will become, why would you ever have anything less than a great attitude? The answer is that there is no reason.

SURVEY SAYS

In order to win, you must expect to win.

If you talk to successful people, you will find out they were successful in their mind before they became successful in reality. Cassius Clay told his mother that he would be the Champion of the World when he was twelve. Neil Armstrong knew at the age of ten he was going to do something great in the field of aviation. I knew I was going to marry Carol the first time I saw her. She was fourteen.

"Where have you been all my life?" I said. She replied, "Teething."

It doesn't matter where you come from but where you're going. Success comes in cans. Failure comes in can'ts.

Treat your body as if it were the only one you will ever have.

Many religions teach that your body is a temple. Most students treat it as an amusement park.

Every time I see a student drunk, or on drugs, or eating ice cream instead of a banana, I see someone whose body will be gone long before it should . . . someone who will be old at fifty . . . and someone who will die much too young. In the fitness business I see people who are young at seventy. People who have shaved ten, twenty, and even thirty years off.

I HAVEN'T GOT TIME FOR THE PAIN

For every hour of exercise you increase your life two hours.

I guess that means if I exercise twelve hours a day I'll live forever. Jonah used to do laps inside of the whale, hoping he'd get pooped out.

It won't be long before science will be able to keep us alive for 150 years or more. How good for those whose bodies are alive, and how bad for those who will have bodies that can't move.

Exercise can not only slow the aging process, it even can reverse it.

He's 110 they say, but doesn't look a day over 100. For his ninetieth birthday his friends decided to surprise him with a hooker. When the sensuous twenty-one-year old arrived at his door, he asked, "What are you doing here?" "I'm here to give you super sex." He thought for a second and said, "I'll take the soup."

There will come a day when we will be able to go to the Parts R Us store and get an artificial or used heart.

That day may not come for those who don't take care of their bodies now. The key to having a good body is simple—you are what you eat and you feel and look as good as you exercise.

Why don't cannibals eat clowns? They taste funny.

SAY KIIIDDS, WHAT TIME IS IT?

A good scare is worth more than advice.

As a freshman at Tech I was introduced to the honor code—I will not lie, cheat, or steal, or condone those who do. This was enforced severely.

One night I was awakened at two A.M. The upperclassmen told us to get into uniform. None of the normal commands were given as we marched to a secluded part of campus. The only sound was the taps of shoes as they clicked on the pavement. It was so dark I could not even see my classmate marching directly in front of me. Four miles later I started to hear a drum. Thu . . . thump! Thu . . . thump! As we got closer to the sound, I saw a light—two large burning torches. Each torch was about ten feet high. Between the two fires I saw someone standing. As I looked out of the corner of my eye, I could see that the entire corp of cadets were being assembled. All two thousand of us.

The drum stopped. Surrounding the torches on all sides were the corps, all directly facing the person standing alone. It was as quiet as an empty church. A loud voice bellowed out the charges. The cadet in the middle had been found guilty of stealing. He was told he was banished forever from Virginia Tech.

I don't recall the words, but my heart was pounding. In a few minutes it was over. The cadet was stripped of his uniform, honor, and dignity. On one command, everyone did an about-face and marched away from the thief.

Go to a few autopsies. Notice the soft pink lungs of the person who never smoked and compare them to the charcoal-black gook caked on the lungs of the smoker. Look at the pure liver of the person who drank water and compare it to the scarred, contracted liver of the person who used alcohol. Ask the doctor for a PET scan of someone who exercised. Compare that with what you see on the scan of a drug user.

You can be scared straight.

A PET scan is not something that will tell how many animal friends you have; rather, it will show the functional areas of the brain.

You don't have to understand anything about medicine to get the message.

DON'T TALK BACK

We are such an arrogant society. Why do we think our ways are the right ways? I believe it is not our place to tell others, with different cultures and beliefs, to do what we want them to do. Talk and reason, sure. Demand, never.

YOU GOT TO KNOW WHEN TO HOLD 'EM

The good poker player will win more often with poor cards than the poor player will win with good cards. So you weren't born into money. So you don't know your parents. You are still in charge of what you will do with your life. The only difference between stumbling blocks and stepping-stones is the way you use them.

Every one of us is given the same amount of time. Time isn't money. It is much more important.

TAKE THIS JOB AND LOVE IT

Once you decide to go to work for someone, it is up to you to give nothing less than your best—all the time. Leave your personal problems in the parking lot. Here are the only words that ever have to come out of your mouth:

Yes.
No.
No excuse.
I'll take care of it.

And if you are asked about a problem, always offer a profitable solution.

EVERYTHING I WANT I HAVE

Why do we always want a little more than we have? Today's extravagance becomes tomorrow's necessity. Why does every horse think his pack is the heaviest? Over half the world's people would trade places with anyone in America.

I complained because I had no shoes until I met a man with no feet.

YOU DON'T KNOW WHAT YOU'VE GOT UNTIL YOU LOSE IT

Bad never seems good until worse happens.

If you take the attitude that you have all you need to make you happy, you will be happy.

HE AIN'T HEAVY

Charlene: All the bachelors being auctioned off have photos and date descriptions in the brochure . . . and then they're paraded in front of us so we can yell out our bids! Bring out the bachelors! I'm ready to shop!!
Cathy: Doesn't it bother you they're not auctioning off any women?
Charlene: Don't be ridiculous. That would be sexist.

Women have control of 70 percent of the wealth in the United States and easy access to the other 30 percent. The remote control is the only power men have left.

CELEBRATE, CELEBRATE, DANCE TO THE MUSIC

No one ever injured his eyesight by looking at the bright side.

You might not live in the best of times, but you can live the best of times. In an unhappy world, you can make your own fun.

I am happy anywhere, doing anything, if I think I am happy. We never know how wonderful the water is until the well runs dry.

SKYROCKETS IN FLIGHT

Beauty is the promise of happiness.

RAINDROPS ON ROSES AND WHISKERS ON KITTENS

There are not many things that will take me away from business, but these are surefire winners:

- My family.
- A hot car. Cars are to men as shopping is to women. While driving through London in our VW, I saw

something I'd never seen before. I stopped. Told Carol I'd be back in a few minutes. A half hour later I returned with the good news—we now own a Lotus.

- A beautiful woman. Which definitely includes my wife. I've always been a pushover for happy eyes and a real smile.
- A secluded walk on the beach.
- A chance to do something new.
- An exhausting workout. Go endorphins go.
- Music. Especially rock and roll.
- Or a good pinball machine. La Crosse is not exactly a major hub for air travel. In order to get anywhere, you have to go through Minneapolis or O'Hare. If I have a choice, I always go through Minneapolis. Their game room is excellent, and they always have the latest pins. The machines in Chicago never work.

WHAT DO YOU MEAN *US*, KEMO SABE?

You can tell what's inside someone by what they laugh at.

Ninety percent of what you worry about will never happen, and most of the remaining 10 percent you can't control . . . so fret not.

WHEN I WAS A BOY AND OLD SHEP WAS A PUP

I always enjoy being around someone at any age, as long as they're still sixteen.

Anyone who is more than fifteen years older than me I consider old. I always defer to someone old.

NINETY MILES AN HOUR DOWN A DEAD END ROAD

Here is one of the dichotomies I have not yet been able to resolve. In order to accomplish great things, you should live today as if you knew you would never die. In order to be happy all the time, you should live today as if you knew you were going to die next month.

To accomplish something great, you need to believe that you will never die.

If you knew you had thirty days to live, wouldn't you spend time with your family? Wouldn't you be as nice to them as you could? And, if you knew you were going to die next week, wouldn't you go ahead and parasail, drive that race car, call up that person you hurt ten years ago and make peace? Wouldn't you put your relationships in order, your life in order, and take those risks you have always wanted to take?

Approach every day as if you only have a month to live and I'll guarantee you two things: a happy life and someday you'll be right.

A journey of a thousand miles must begin with a single step. And most great things are more than a thousand miles. If you think you will never die and you believe you will be able to take all of the steps to accomplish great things, you will.

How have I been able to resolve this dichotomy? Not very well. I try to handle my family life as though I were going to die tomorrow, and my business life as though I were going to live forever. Sometimes I forget.

YOU CAN'T PLEASE EVERYONE, SO YOU'VE GOT TO PLEASE YOURSELF

Nothing seems like work if we want to do it. Everything seems like slavery if we don't. The only difference is our attitude.

If you don't like something, you have three choices: change it, walk away, or change your attitude. What do you do if you find yourself with a negative person? Keep nice. Keep polite. Keep moving.

CHICKENNNN . . . MANNNNN, HE'S EVERYWHERE, HE'S EVERYWHERE

There is opportunity everywhere, even in the worst of circumstances. The Chinese say it best. Their language is composed of over 50,000 symbols. The word for "crisis" in Chinese is composed of two symbols . . . the first means "danger," the second "opportunity." The only problem with opportunity is it usually looks like a problem or hard work, so most of us don't recognize it. I don't have to create an opportunity—I just have to be smart enough to see one when it's there.

If I see an opportunity, I try to treat it as one. If I see a threat, I treat it as though it were an opportunity just wearing a disguise.

GONNA MAKE IT HAPPEN

There isn't much luck in this world. You create your own luck.

Far better to be prepared for an opportunity that never comes than to meet an opportunity and not be prepared.

Luck is when we have the preparation to recognize, seize, and meet an opportunity.

Destiny is not a matter of chance, it is a matter of choice.

AIN'T NO MOUNTAIN HIGH ENOUGH

The turtle only makes progress when he sticks his neck out.

The greatest mistake one can make in life is to live as though we are afraid to make one. If you talk to older people who are about to die and ask them what they would have done differently if they could go back and change their lives, one of the most frequent responses has to do with taking more risks. Failure is merely an opportunity to start over again, wiser than before.

CREATURES KEEP ON CREATCHING

You get older, but you don't have to get old. Most people are dead long before they die. It is a lot better to wear out than rust out. Life is either dangerous or it is boring, and scared is better than bored. On the ledge, but not over the edge.

Make sure when you get ready to die you don't look back and say "I didn't live."

Life is meant for living.

ANOTHER PAGE OF HISTORY TURNED AND THE BEAT GOES ON

It does appear the only lesson history has taught us is that we don't seem to learn anything from it. Every one of us believes we will not make the same mistakes the person before us made. Not true.

When I was young, it didn't seem important to be

living in Hawaii right after World War II. It was no big deal when Robert Kennedy came over to visit my parents when we lived in Virginia. Even as a young adult, it didn't seem like history to be in the army from 1967 to 1970—it just seemed like a difficult time.

Somewhere in your life you realize when history is being made, and it is exciting to be part of it. I'm not sure when the transition from ignorance to realization takes place, but I wish I had recognized it when I was young.

When you're young, history just doesn't seem like history when you are going through it.

LUCY MUST KNOW THAT THE WORLD IS FLAT 'CAUSE WHEN SOMEONE LEAVES TOWN THEY NEVER COME BACK

See the nine dots below. Go through all nine dots by using four straight lines. Oh, by the way, once you start you can't lift up your pencil.

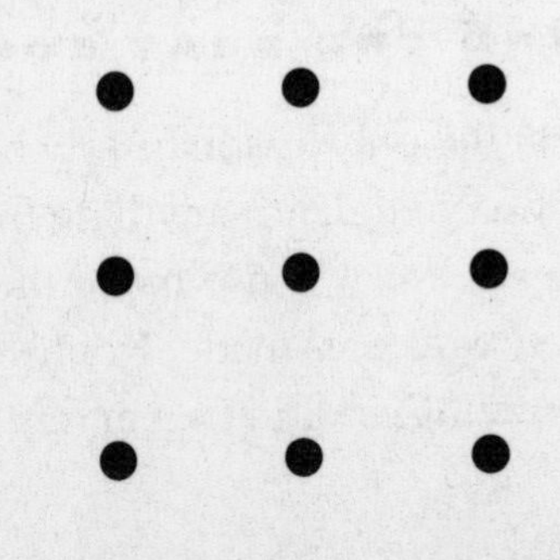

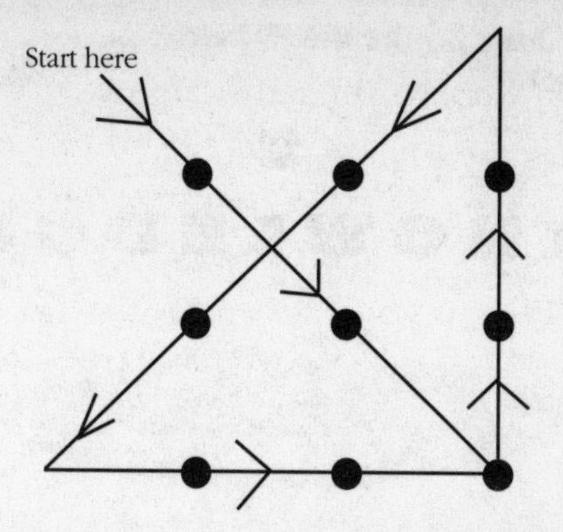

The answer is easy once you realize you are no longer confined by the natural border all of us see around the exterior of the dots.

It is tough to think beyond conditioning.

It's amazing what one can accomplish if one doesn't know it can't be done. Thinking it can be done is the same as knowing it can be done, but if we think there is a glass ceiling, we will forever be confined below it.

Knowing it can be done is half the battle.

THE BIG LESSONS

To get a great attitude, just pretend you have one. You become what you believe you will become.

Oz never did give anything to the tin man that he didn't already have.

2 KNOWLEDGE

There are so many things I always thought were beyond my comprehension. Thermodynamics . . . the Paris subway schedule . . . changing the time on my VCR clock. I've found nothing is very difficult to learn if I want to learn it. We are all ignorant about different things.

> **Everything is easy once you know how.**

DON'T KNOW WHAT A SLIDE RULE IS FOR

When you talk, you only say something you already know. When you listen, you may learn what someone else knows. Having nothing to say seldom stops anyone from saying it.

We were given one mouth and two ears so we can listen twice as much as we talk. It is better to know some of the questions than all of the answers. If you ask a few wrong questions, you'll get the wrong answers. However, if all you do is ask questions, eventually you will know the answers.

Most people will agree with you if you'll just keep quiet. It is best to keep your mouth shut all the time and let everyone think you are a fool than to say something and remove all doubt. You never have to explain something you haven't said.

ATTENTION, KMART SHOPPERS

We are all saving ourselves for the senior prom. Many of us forget that somewhere along the line we have to learn to dance. There is no better definition of the dance than knowledge.

HEARD IT THROUGH THE GRAPEVINE

You only really know the road if you have traveled it.

Books are nice. They give you a chance to learn from the mistakes of others—and that's good because you can never live long enough to make all of them yourself. But you really only know what it is like to load the dock if you have done it—you can only learn so much from class.

I don't know how they conduct basic training today, but when Vietnam was going on, the army got you used to being shot at by shooting at you.

In the middle of a pitch-black night, we were taken to a football field. At one end someone was given a machine gun with red tracer bullets. We were at the other end. We were then told to get on our stomachs and crawl toward the fire.

We got so nervous, we were giving the victory sign with just one finger.

Watching red tracer bullets a foot or two above your head, while crawling and clutching the dirt, does get your attention. Experience is something you just can't learn in the classroom.

The phrase "heard it through the grapevine" is not from the California raisins. During the Civil War the news was telegraphed to and from the front. When the army moved, there wasn't time to build telegraph poles, so they strung the wire from tree to tree. The wire came in coils, like a Slinky. As they uncoiled the wire and put it in the trees, it looked like a grapevine. The news was something that was "heard through the grapevine."

STUDYING HARD, HOPING TO PASS

Education dictates your station in life. Even though you may not think you use all the material you have learned, just the confidence you gain

Education gives you the confidence to know you have something to fall back on.

knowing you have an education is worth more than everything you actually know.

The fool doth think he is wise, but the wise man knows himself to be a fool.

People may be uneducated, but they are not stupid.

I remember an elder tribesman, from a remote village in the middle of nowhere in Brazil, saying, "These trees are the lungs of the world." He may have been uneducated, but he was certainly not stupid.

I can't say the reverse is true. I've been to a lot of campuses and have seen many very well educated people, some of whom are not very bright.

Long whiskers cannot take the place of brains.

I THINK YOU'LL UNDERSTAND

Consider this educated response to a problem. Suppose you owned one airplane that had one hundred seats. You were fortunate enough to sell all hundred seats for every flight. At that level of sales, you were bringing in enough money to pay for the plane, the fuel, the pilots, the flight attendants, food, insurance, and other operating costs. As a matter of fact, you could even afford to pay for a few extras.

Now, let's also assume each person on the flight only paid two thirds of the cost of their ticket; the other third was paid for by a benevolent friend.

The friend calls you up and says, instead of paying for 33 percent of the ticket he is going to pay a little less. As the owner you decide you need to take action. Which of the following would you do?

a. Tell fifteen people to get off the plane.
b. Increase the number of flight attendants.
c. Pay the pilot and flight attendants more money.
d. All of the above.

If you picked *d,* you could run the University of Wisconsin in La Crosse.

A few years ago we had 10,000 students. Each student paid about two thirds of what the university said were the costs. The state picked up the other third. The state decided it was no longer going to pay the third, but somewhat less.

What did the university do?

a. It told people to get off the plane. Today we have 8,500 students.
b. It increased the number of flight attendants. Today we have more faculty with 8,500 students than we had with 10,000 students.

c. It increased the pay of the pilot and the flight attendants. Not only do we have more faculty, but their pay is much higher.

Come on, Swayne, they must have:

- Torn down some buildings? Nope.
- At least closed down some buildings? Negative.
- Reduced the number of administrative staff? Ha!
- Cut down total costs somewhere? Fat chance.
- Recruited out-of-state students who have to pay their full fee? No.
- Raised tuition prices? A little.
- Cried to the legislature to get more from the taxpayer? Yep! As this is being written, the U is getting ready to spend over $15 million to upgrade and expand its facilities.

One of the regents was kind enough to look this over. He explained the rationale of some of these moves. If quality is defined as a better teacher-to-student ratio, then to increase quality you increase the number of faculty and decrease the number of students. To me that makes good "quality" sense, but not a lot of "financial" sense.

AS I WALK ALONG I WONDER WHAT WENT WRONG

There is a simple way for universities in financial trouble to get out, and they don't have to raise the price of tuition.

What is it? Fire half of all the professors. Then tell the other half they are going to have to double their teaching load.

THE NEW WORLD ORDER

Another improvement necessary is to get rid of all the Twinkie courses. Credits for bowling, surfing, sleeping (yes, one college offers a class where the students get credit for sleeping), snowboarding, and Frisbee?

Two workers in the back room of a bakery would pass the time throwing pie plates back and forth. The name of the bakery was etched on the plates—Mrs. Frisbee's.

How many physical education majors does it take to screw in a light bulb? One, but he gets three credits for it.

I'LL BUY A VOWEL

Give a man a fish and you feed him for a day . . . teach a man to fish and you feed him for a lifetime.

Some professors say you can lead a man to the university, but you can't make him think. I disagree. My overriding philosophy of teaching is if a student hasn't learned, the teacher hasn't taught.

TO MOW OR TO GROW

It's not easy to find weeds in your lawn, but it can be done. Tear up the entire lawn. The things that grow back—those are the weeds.

Some of my classes have fewer than forty students, but most have many more. It's tough to identify the weeds in the big classes. I use the following approach. The poor student will drop out because of the work. We certainly don't want anyone to ever have a failing grade, so the U lets students drop months after the class has begun.

The average student will be overwhelmed with the work, the good student will be challenged, the excellent student will find the class too easy—that's the only rub with a big class.

Thoughts, like fleas, jump from person to person, but they don't bite everyone.

If someone tells me something, or I've read it, I usually put it into my long-term memory if I think it was very interesting or I might be able to use it someday. Even then, I forget a lot.

There are only a few ways I know of to make sure people remember something. One is by repetition. I can still recite a lot of patter my parents forced me to memorize when I was five.

Another is a traumatic event. Even today, over forty years later, I can recall vividly everything—every smell, every sound, every picture—the day I saw my dog die.

A third way is by discovery. Experience is a perfect way to get things into a student's brain so that it never leaves. If I discover something, I have learned it.

I also realize the discovery method is frustrating to many. Recently I took some college students to Europe for a month.

Experience is the comb nature gives us when we are bald.

Even though I had lived in Europe, I pretended I knew nothing. I made them order off the menu. I made them change the money. I made them figure out how to use the train system. I made them conduct their own walkabout.

It is common for college-age Australians to take a year and backpack around the world; they call this adventure their "walkabout."

On that European trip, we rented a van in Munich, wanting to go to Salzburg. As touristy as it sounds, I still enjoy the *Sound of Music* tour. One of the students was assigned navigation duty and, instead of three hours, it took the entire day. They knew how Gilligan felt.

We ended up in the wrong country. Every student was at their mental edge. Not only were they yelling at the navigator, they were going bonkers with each other. Young women certainly do have a potty mouth these days.

You should have heard the cheer when the navigator announced, "Hey, we're back on the map."

By the end of the first week, most wanted to go home—for good. But a funny thing happened along the way. By the end of the third week, they had learned how to get along. By the last week, every one of them had gained the confidence to go to any country. Without realizing it, they made the transition from knowledge to wisdom.

Knowledge comes, but wisdom lingers.

I hear. I forget.
I see. I remember.
I do. I understand.

I also think they will remember the trip for the rest of their lives—the smell of cat urine in Venice; mountain biking in the Alps; the Stones concert in the Munich Olympic Village; and watching Checkpoint Charlie being taken down. They found out more about life and themselves in one month than they had in four years in the classroom.

The only time I ever interfered was when I thought they would get hurt. At two A.M. in the Amsterdam red-light district, I told the women we should not go into one of the live shows. I didn't let them drive in any city.

I was the one who put the red racing stripe on our white van when I came too close to a parked red VW. If the owner of the VW reads this, I apologize—I thought the "thud" was the students in the back of the van fooling around. When they told me what had happened, it was too late. I was caught in traffic and couldn't turn around. I owe you a paint job.

THE CANARY IN THE MINE SHAFT

The wisest people follow their own direction. Still, wise people are not wise all the time. If you are keeping your head while everyone else is losing theirs, there is the possibility you have not truly grasped the situation.

Once you have had many experiences, you do become wise.

My first Christmas in La Crosse, 1970, I discovered one could cut one's own tree. I therefore suggested to Carol that we go do that. A little family togetherness never hurt anyone. So we took the three little ones and headed out to discover nature—raw and cold!

What do you do if Santa gets stuck in your chimney? Use Santiflush.

After trouncing through the snow with everyone picking a different tree, we settled on the one *I* liked best. Carol said it looked a little big. I assured her it was perfect. One hour later it was cut—for another hour we tugged and pulled and got it to the car. It took another twenty minutes to get it on top of the car and strap it down. We couldn't even see out of the side or back windows of our VW station wagon. We had to tie the branches back in the front so I could see to drive.

That is when I should have realized it was too big. But no.

An hour later, when we got home, we discovered it would not fit through the front door—or the double back door. So I cut off some branches. It still wouldn't fit. Out again—I cut off half the top. Then, it barely fit. But when we got it in, I accidentally poked the top of the tree through the ceiling.

By this time the tree didn't even look like a tree. It was full from floor to ceiling and took up the entire living room. We couldn't get in or out the front door. Carol never said a word.

From then on I let Carol pick out the trees.

I RAN ALL THE WAY HOME

Hopefully, you are graduating from a university that has taught you how to think, not what to think. Also, how to handle difficulty. If your parents or university have taught you to handle obstacles, future ones won't seem tough.

You are going to be insulted, cheated, fired, divorced, mugged—and then it gets worse.

If you have been taught how to be a success, then you know how to handle setbacks and unpleasant situations, not duck from them. Tough times don't last. Tough people do. If it doesn't kill you, it makes you stronger. The strongest steel must go through the hottest fire.

WHO WOULD YOU RATHER HAVE AS YOUR SIDEKICK, KIM OR ROBIN?

Common sense is as rare as genius.

Don't confuse knowledge with common sense. The more experiences you have, the more common sense means something.

IN THE LAND OF THE BLIND THE ONE-EYED MAN IS KING

They can't take away things from between your ears. Education really is your best investment. So you go belly-up. So you lose everything. So what? What you know is power, and the more you know the more powerful you become.

Better an empty wallet than an empty head.

POETRY IN MOTION, DANCING CLOSE TO ME

Everything I can learn, anyone can learn, but my heart is my own.

THE BIG LESSON

Luck is where preparation meets opportunity. Learning is the preparation.

The team was so proud of their second place finish they had their silver medals bronzed.

3 RESPONSIBILITY

You are responsible for everything you do or fail to do.

YOU KNOW IT DON'T COME EASY

With your children, or your employees, you are also responsible for everything they do or fail to do.

THAT'S A VERY NICE DRESS YOU HAVE ON, MRS. CLEAVER

You never have a second chance to make a first impression. Proper grooming and great clothes open all doors.

Barbara Billingsley wore pearls much of the time because she had a scar on her throat.

The best impressions are not flashy. Everyone admires quiet class. If you have it, you will stand out far above the ostentatious.

You may delegate authority . . . but you can't delegate responsibility.

Initiative is doing the right thing without being told. Underpromise and overdeliver. Pretend every report you write, every briefing you make, everything you do is being watched by the chairman of the board. You will be recognized immediately as a pro.

BILLIE JOE NEVER HAD A LICK OF SENSE, PASS THE BISCUITS, PLEASE

CEOs didn't learn good manners after they became CEOs. They knew how to act, and somewhere along the line they were unexpectedly put in a position where they impressed someone with their demeanor.

I TOUCH NO ONE AND NO ONE TOUCHES ME

I don't tell my next-door neighbor how to live—as long as his actions don't impact me or those I care about, I leave him alone.

INSTEAD OF GOOD ADVICE, THEY ARE JUST MAKING VICE LOOK GOOD

I'm not a Crusader Rabbit. I don't bother people in our society who have sick behavior. I vote with my feet.

IN THE DESERT YOU CAN'T REMEMBER YOUR NAME

You know the kind of person who when he can't dance blames the unevenness of the floor? The one who claims the cards are not shuffled properly, unless of course he gets a good hand? Reasons are excuses, and excuses are unacceptable. There are no excuses for someone with a responsible attitude.

If you want the rainbow, you've got to put up with the rain.

THE BIG LESSON

The price of greatness is responsibility. You are the only one responsible for what you do.

4
INTEGRITY

The Ten Commandments are a good place to start.

YOUR MISSION, SHOULD YOU DECIDE TO ACCEPT IT . . .

The first three commandments tell us how we should behave toward God. The last seven tell us how we should behave toward each other. It is a list of nots. No killing, stealing, lying, envy, or cheating on your spouse.

All of those commandments apply to acts that are forbidden. It seemed to me it would have been better to say the commandments in a positive tone. "Respect life" instead of "no killing."

The reason I always like things said positively is because it is difficult for the mind to picture a *not.* If I tell you not to think of a pink elephant driving a

Corvette, your mind instantly pictures what I just told you not to picture.

Then, I noticed most laws all around the world revolve around these commandments. Thousands of years after we were introduced to these commandments, they are still accepted as law everywhere.

It's obvious God can see into the future better than I can.

The only commandment said in the positive is one that isn't law, the one many societies have forgotten: "Honor Mom and Dad."

TEACHER IS TEACHING THE GOLDEN RULE

Remember the documentary movie *History of the World*? Moses came down from the mountain with three tablets. Each tablet had five commandments. He walked up to the crowd and proclaimed, "Come see the fifteen . . ." One of the tablets slipped from his hand, breaking on the ground. "Make that ten commandments."

Maybe not. But if there were five more, here's one that would have been included: Treat everyone—your customer, employee, family, boss—exactly as you would want to be treated if you were that person.

Hey, this isn't the golden rule . . . not exactly. As long as the person is similar to you, the "treat everyone as you would like to be treated" holds. But if they have a different personality, background, culture, or set of values, then you should take the extra step of trying to put yourself in their shoes. You will find some do want to be treated differently than you would, and when you use empathy to at least attempt to understand them, you take the golden rule platinum.

LIES! LIES! I CAN'T BELIEVE A WORD YOU SAY

The greatest truths are simple. Perhaps the greatest of the truths is truth itself. It is always the strongest argument. You don't have to have a good memory if you tell the truth—you sure don't have to remember what you told or to whom. Whatever will come out eventually must come out immediately.

Truth withstands every test. It fears no trial.

The best thing about telling the truth is you feel good about it. I always try to tell the truth, although I admit I lie to save someone's feelings. Even though the dinner was bad, I'd never tell that to a host.

YOU KEEP LYING WHEN YOU SHOULD BE TRUTHIN'

At times I don't tell all the truth. When dealing with those I don't trust, I won't lie to them, but if I don't want to answer something, I just tell them that I'm not going to tell them the answer. Many times if they haven't asked the right question, I don't volunteer the answer I know they are looking for. In general, truth works out to be the best, and it sure makes living easier.

OKLAHOMA SOONERS

We all know situations when the liar seemed to have won. But they only win on that day.

When honor is involved, be deaf to expediency.

Remember those old westerns when everyone lined up with their buckboards and waited for the starting gun so they could race to claim the land they wanted? That's the way it was supposed to work. But almost all of the claims filed in Oklahoma were filed by those who snuck ahead of those waiting at the starting line. The landowners were known as "sooners" because they got to the land sooner than those who played fair.

I FEEL GOOD, I KNEW THAT I WOULD

Having been in business for over twenty-five years, I can flat out guarantee you dealing honestly and with integrity are the absolute best ways to enjoy your prosperity.

NO U-TURN EXCEPT FOR AUTHORIZED VEHICLES

Our town is so small you don't have to use your car's turn indicator because everyone knows where you're going. Well, not quite—but that's just how it is in your business community.

Once you've been around a few years, you won't need to use your business' turn indicator. Your customers, employees, and competitors will know where you're going. If you haven't established a reputation for telling the truth, no one will believe you—even when you *are* telling the truth.

I BET YOU'RE WONDRIN' HOW I KNEW

If you aren't a thief, then you need to be able to tell who is straight and who isn't.

The thief thinks everyone steals.

The eyes are the window to the truth.

Here's a technique that works much more than it doesn't:

In our society it is considered proper to look each other in the eye. (Which is not true, by the way, in many other societies.) When you ask someone a question, watch their eyes carefully. If they look straight into your eyes, they are telling the truth. If they are right-handed, and look off to the right briefly and then look you in the eye, they are being honest. (Likewise, if they are left-handed, and look off to the left and then look you in the eye, they are truthful.)

If they look up, it means they are trying to remember. Usually they are replaying a scene in their mind. After they look up and then look at you, they are also telling the truth.

However, if they are right-handed and look to the left, they are usually lying (or if they are left-handed and look to the right). Or if they look down, even briefly, they are usually being dishonest. Unfortunately, a good con man can overcome this with practice.

DON'T EAT THE YELLOW SNOW

The heart knows long before the head does.

If it looks bad, smells bad, or you have bad vibes, walk away. I have never, absolutely never, been in a relationship or business arrangement that worked out when I felt something "wrong" in my subconscious. It doesn't matter how good the deal looks on paper. When you look at the other person, if it doesn't feel right, trust your instinct. Walk away.

When you lie down with a dog you get fleas.

WE MAY NEVER PASS THIS WAY AGAIN

Fool me once, shame on you. Fool me twice, shame on me.

I can be fooled. Even though I think I'm a fair judge of people, I've been snookered. Once someone does it to me, I should have learned my lesson, and it usually doesn't happen a second time. If you allow it to happen a second time, you are almost as guilty as the fooler.

If you break your leg in two places, stop going to those places.

For sure, it never happens to me a third time.

WHEN I WAS JUST A BOY, THE DEVIL CALLED MY NAME

There are not many people who have lived a lot who can say they haven't done things they regret—and I certainly fall into that category. There was a time in my youth when, if I had to pick between two evils, I picked the one I hadn't tried before. It was the time in my life when I could resist everything except temptation.

Thou shall not commit adultery. Thou shall not covet thy neighbor's wife. I'm glad my name's not Thou.

DEVIL WITH A BLUE DRESS ON

Now I know that when I have to pick between two evils, whatever I choose is still evil. Where does the ant die? In the sugar.

TWO THUMBS DOWN

Everyone is a moon, and has a dark side which he never shows to anybody. The side of us that is evil. For some it is almost natural to live in the dark and terrible rooms in their mind's house. Many of us walk the line. The problem is, while it is easy to slip over, it is difficult to get back.

OTHER THAN THAT, MRS. LINCOLN ENJOYED THE PLAY IMMENSELY

A whole society can move over to the dark side. The most awful acts don't seem so bad when they become everyday occurrences.

KNOCK KNOCK KNOCKIN' ON HEAVEN'S DOOR

When you are getting ready to do something you know is wrong, isn't it strange you feel like someone is watching? You may think this is wacko, but I believe someone really is watching. It is either a group of your past generations or future generations.

If it's your past generations, this would be something God decided would be a good way for them to spend their time. Instead of field trips, they should go around to all of their offspring and try to keep them doing the right thing.

THE SHADOW KNOWS

Could it possibly be future generations? Absolutely! Time is just a place. It is not something that is here now and gone in the next instant. Time travel is not only possible, it occurs every time we send an astronaut into space. If an astronaut takes a watch with him, when he returns his clock is a few seconds slower than it would have been had he stayed on earth and he is a few seconds younger than if he had stayed on earth. If you have had a lot of physics, then you know all about this. If you haven't, just accept the concept for the moment. You can go ask one of the professors in the physics department if you think I'm wrong.

Time is relative . . . it is a place . . . and time travel is possible.

HOW CAN I BE SURE, IN A WORLD THAT'S CONSTANTLY CHANGING?

When there is no law, there is conscience.

Just maybe your past or future generations are standing right next to you cheering or booing everything you do. When you get ready to do something wrong, they are the voices in your head doing everything in their power to get you to behave like a great-great-grandson (or great-great-grandfather) should. They can't stop you; they can just stand over you like a dark cloud, hoping you'll get the message.

A PETE MARAVICH PASS

You can tell a lot about someone's integrity if you can play some games with them—especially if those games are one-on-one. Everyone's true character comes through when they compete.

THE BIG LESSON

Those who try to be everything to everybody end up being nothing to anyone. Deep down they become shallow.

If you don't stand for something, you'll fall for anything. How do you make sure what you do is honest and right?

Just assume whatever you do is being watched by your spouse, your children, or your parents, and will appear tomorrow on the front page of the newspaper. That's enough to keep me in line. Most of the time.

After his episode with the inflatable doll, I'm sure the Thanksgiving parade will never be the same.

5
GOD

Us, the world, the universe . . . this is one of the few things both sides of my brain agree on.

DON'T BE CONCERNED. IT WILL NOT HARM YOU. IT'S ONLY ME PURSUING SOMETHING I'M NOT SURE OF

There has to be God. This didn't just happen.

Did you know the entire universe is expanding? You probably did know that. But, did you know the universe is expanding at exactly the same speed in every direction, and the center of the expansion appears to be the earth? What does that mean?

THOUGH IT'S ALWAYS CROWDED, YOU STILL CAN FIND SOME ROOM

I'm not so sure a God that creates all that is can be overly concerned with my everyday life. I'll trust in God, but I'll also cut the cards and tie my camel.

It sure is curious how a lot of people all of a sudden believe in God when faced with danger but lose their faith after the crisis has past.

I've never found an atheist in a foxhole.

The Supreme Court temporarily lifts the ban on prayer during earthquakes and hurricanes.

I BELIEVE FOR EVERY DROP OF RAIN THAT FALLS

I'm a Catholic. With all the religions in the world, how can I be sure mine is the right one? I can't. The Catholic Church used to be a beacon for me, but as it has become watered down, it has become more like a distant candle flickering in the mist.

Religion is the anchor of morality.

If you believe in God, it is a lot easier to accept a set of principled morals. If you live by those morals, and if there is a God and a heaven, then maybe you do have a chance to live forever. Faith must be believing what you know just can't be.

THE BIG LESSONS

We all need stability, and in your lifetime you will find the only possible sources of constancy are your family and God.

The real bottom line must be heaven. God will look at the clean hands, not the full ones.

6 LIVING

Life is a lot more than increasing its speed.

GIVE ME JUST A LITTLE MORE TIME

The day you were born, an hourglass was tipped over with your name on it. The gamble is how much sand is in it. But we are all equal because no matter what we do, we can't make the hole smaller or push the sand back in.

Better to go into every building on campus and sit in a class you know nothing about at least once than to go to the same building and see the same professors and the same students all the time. Better to hike up Pilatus (you'll never forget it and the room at the top is not expensive) than to take the cable car. Better to know your grandparents well by spending a week alone with them than only a few hours on a holiday. Better to be engaged for a year than to marry quickly.

You'll never know how easy the shot might have been until you visit the Texas School Book Depository.

TIME CAN DO SO MUCH

When you graduate, you think you have all the time in the world. Then one day you wake up and you find fifty years have passed. Time wasted today cannot be recaptured tomorrow.

Some may start the race ahead or behind others. Yet if we use our time well, our life will be great. You may say you should spend your time getting ready for the future. I disagree. Some spend too much time getting ready to live, but never really living. Worse are those who never worry about tomorrow, just today.

Yin and yang. Balance.

Today is the tomorrow you worried about yesterday. It is far better to live today for today, even while you are preparing for the future.

Not understand that? Sure, you do have to learn some things for tomorrow, but the point is, as you are getting ready for tomorrow, you can enjoy today.

TELL THE TEACHER WE'RE SURFIN'

If you spend all your time preparing for the future, when the future finally comes, you'll find it far less satisfying than you had imagined.

We are always getting ready to live, but never living.

THE F WORD . . . FUN

I'm sure you know one half of your brain is for logic and the other half is for emotion. When your emotion says one thing and logic says another, go with your heart. Life turns out to be much more fun that way.

Those who study the brain say we use only about 10 percent of it. Did you ever consider they have a 90 percent chance of being wrong?

Everything you need to see can be seen by your heart. Nothing worth seeing is just seen by your eyes.

CRYING OVER YOU

Unfortunately, part of life is depression. The only way to learn how to handle it is to go through it.

Someday we will be able to have "experiences" implanted into our brain. We will then be able to handle almost anything. Until then, we've got to go through it.

WHEN THE DOG BITES, WHEN THE BEE STINGS

The first rule of holes. If you find yourself in one, stop digging. It is tough when a loved one dies, you get fired, or get a divorce, and twice as tough if the troubles are self-inflicted. But usually the sorrow passes. A common way to hide suffering is to throw yourself into work. This helps mask the symptoms, but takes a long time to soothe the cause.

BLUER THAN BLUE

Unfortunately, sometimes the grief seems like it won't go away. When that happens, you have to get it out. You can either get it out by using your mind or taking action. Self-hypnosis, meditation, mind control, and deep relaxation are all essentially the same. What they can do is allow you to mend a difficulty.

GOTTA START A NEW LIFE

Or, you can take action. You can't get new parents, but you can find new friends. You can't get your old job back, but you can find a new one. You can't, or may not want to, get your spouse back, but you can find someone new.

THE BIG LESSON

Enjoy today while preparing for tomorrow.

7 FAMILY

There is nothing more important in my life than my family. You hear the phrase "family values" a lot these days. It just means you value your family.

DOOR NUMBER 2 OR BACHELORETTE NUMBER 3

I married the most beautiful woman I ever met. I'm not just saying that to cover myself when she reads this.

OH! CAROL

As I said before, we got married way too young. Carol and I had our first child when she was nineteen and I had just turned twenty-one. When I see my students, or our children at that age, I realize now we were children when we got married. We were still infants when we started having children. We should have put a snooze button on our biological clock.

Treat, don't cheat.

THE CAT'S IN THE CRADLE

The first few years in my business I worked eighty plus hours a week, fifty-two weeks a year. Even so, it is the type of business where you get to see your children all the time. They got the opportunity to clean toilets, vacuum the tennis courts, and in general find out what work is really like. I'm grateful I had the chance to combine a career with my children.

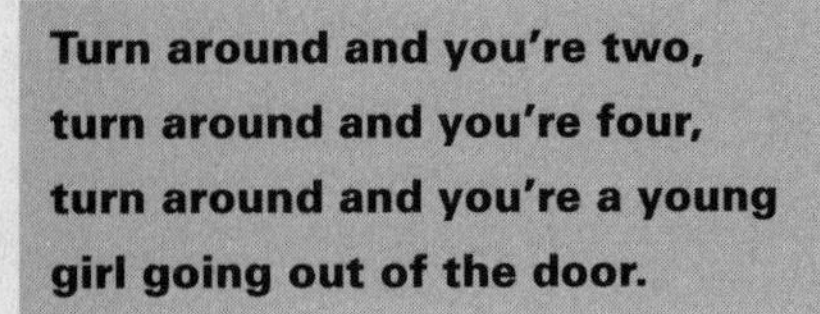

RING RING GOES THE BELL

When Joe was in the eighth grade, we tried the home school approach. Carol took on the social studies and language subjects, I did the science and field trips. Every Wednesday I would take Joe on a field trip, doing the things I always wanted to do—a full day at the go-cart track at Wisconsin Dells for driving lessons; a visit to a houseboat factory; a tour of a business

Not every teacher is a parent, but every parent is a teacher.

that makes the biggest plastic animals you have ever seen.

The trip I remember most was taking him flying. Small plane. Very windy day. Joe and the pilot sat in the two front seats—Carol and I were scrunched down in the back. You should have seen the terrified look on Carol's face when Joe took over the controls and the plane started to dive. Very educational!

I also wanted to teach Joe about the stock market. So I entered him in a national computer game for those who play the stock market. I also entered myself and a friend of mine, who went bankrupt when the oil depression hit.

After eight weeks, Dad—that was me, the person who wrote a book on the stock market—and my friend, the former oil millionaire, were well behind Joe in the game. Joe came in first simply buying stocks that made products he liked.

It reminded me of the day six-year-old Tracy took five-week-old Joe to school for "show and tell." Guess who "showed and told" in the stock market game? Sometimes the student is the teacher.

The genes are yours. That's the heredity. The home is yours. That's the environment.

If the kids look like Dad, that's heredity . . . if they look like a neighbor's dad, that's environment.

As a teacher, the most important books you can read to your children are *The Little Engine That Could* and the Bible. You want to make sure they have wings and roots.

I'm convinced a child's basic personality is 95 percent heredity. However, I'm also convinced you can train their young branches to point toward the sun. You have the most important influence on how your children use their personality and whether they develop an honorable character. The apples don't fall far from the tree.

MOTHER KANGAROOS HATE RAINY WEATHER. THE KIDS HAVE TO PLAY INSIDE.

Until your children become adults, you are their parent, not their friend. You are not their brother or sister, but their teacher and leader.

Discipline is not suppression. Discipline builds inner confidence. You can have empathy for what they are going through, but empathy should seldom become sympathy.

Discipline is the act of teaching things that need to be ingrained on their teleprompter of life.

High expectations, high results. Low expectations, low results. High expectations require making them sweat through difficult situations without Mom or Dad.

Working through a hardship is something they will remember, and it will influence them the rest of their lives. Almost as important, is how fast they learn when faced with adversity. Storms make trees take deeper roots.

BRIGHT ARE THE STARS THAT SHINE, DARK IS THE SKY

Never punish if your children have given their best, whether in a task or in competition. If they lose, make sure you talk with them. Find out what they learned from their loss. You really can learn to win tomorrow, if you know why you lost today. It is your difficult responsibility to strike a tough balance between making sure they are challenged and putting them in a position where they have a chance to win. Neither your children nor you will ever know how much they can do unless they are challenged. There is no real success unless they have the freedom to fail.

PUT ME IN, COACH, I'M READY TO PLAY . . . TODAY

It's good when they start to win. Even though they can learn some things from losing, they learn a lot more, and become more, by winning. Childhood memories last for the long haul. There is no feeling like the feeling of success, especially when you are young. When you win, nothing hurts.

KEEP ME SEARCHING FOR A HEART OF GOLD . . . AND I'M GETTING OLD

Punish for acts of dishonor.

When handing out punishment for an act not really dishonorable, but that nevertheless requires your action, take a day before making a decision.

When Brian was twelve and Tracy ten, they went out skiing with an adult friend of the family. Brian and Tracy were told to be home by eight P.M., but if they couldn't make it, they were to call and let us know.

When it was obvious they were going to be late, they tried to get to a phone to call us. They couldn't. Then they asked our adult friend to call us. He told them that he would. He didn't!

WHAT WE HAVE HERE IS A FAILURE TO COMMUNICATE

By eleven P.M. we were very worried. I took off and scoured the town. I came back at one A.M. to see if they were home yet. They weren't.

At two A.M. they came home. They were laughing and having a great time as our friend dropped them off at the front door. I didn't ask for any explanation. As they walked in the door, I was so mad I said, "You are grounded for a year!" Tracy said, "But, Dad . . ." I yelled, "Make that two years!" Brian told her to shut up, otherwise it would be for life.

Even though I found out later what the story was, I told them it was their responsibility to make sure we were called, not someone else's. I regret to this day making the mistake of handing out such a punishment when I was angry. I hadn't known the whole story, but it was also important they knew when Mom or Dad said something, we meant it.

Brian and Tracy *were* grounded for two years.

I CAN'T WAIT FOREVER, TIME WON'T LET ME

A boy becomes an adult three years before his father thinks he does and about two years after he thinks he does. A boy never becomes an adult to his mother.

Chuck, our son who played professional tennis, has traveled all around the world, by himself, for the last ten years. He has been in five earthquakes, in three countries as coup attempts were happening, in Israel when they were fighting, stranded in countries without any money, and flew Kuwait Airlines a few days before Hussein invaded. He has been through more in the last few years than most go through in a lifetime. But when he comes home, Carol still waits up for him, he still has a curfew, and he still kisses his mom good night.

It is better for your children to waste their youth than to do nothing with it at all.

STUCK INSIDE THESE FOUR WALLS, TRAPPED INSIDE FOREVER

Children have no idea how they are treating their parents.

I began college very young—at sixteen. At the end of my sophomore year, I was so bored and restless I announced to my parents I was going to hitchhike around the United States. I'm sure they didn't believe me. I left our home in Virginia in early June with less than ten dollars in my pocket and a suitcase with "California, Please" taped on the side.

My note to my parents was short: "Gone hitchhiking—be back in a few months. Love, son." They knew which son it was and that I didn't have any money. Looking back, I know they must have been worried.

As I made my way across the United States, the little money I made I spent making sure I always had a haircut and my clothes were clean. I seldom had to wait more than ten minutes before someone would give me another ride.

I sent my parents a postcard at least twice a week. I also managed to always get a meal and a place to stay by walking up anyplace and saying, "I don't have any money. If you will give me a meal, I'll spend two hours doing any job you want." I used the same approach in finding a place to stay. No problems—ever.

GOT ON BOARD A WESTBOUND 747

As I was working my way through California, I stopped in San Diego and liked it. So, I stayed for a few weeks. I got a job as an ice cream truck driver. At the end of my first two weeks, I received a paycheck—$102. I picked up a newspaper and saw the ad "$99 air fare to Hawaii one way. Plane leaves at midnight tonight." There was no decision to be made. Naturally, I was on that plane, and with $3 left over.

HELLO, MUDDUH, HELLO, FADDAH. HERE I AM AT . . .

On the flight I met a young Japanese woman, my age, who was on her way to Tokyo. I had a few leftover postcards from California and she had cards she had brought from Japan. We traded. I wrote on one of her Japanese postcards my parents' address and a profound message, "Great country, but I can't speak the language." I then asked her to mail it when she got to Japan.

As soon as I landed in Hawaii, I sent my parents a card. I'm sure it must have been a shock. A few days later, they received the card from Japan. To this day I've always wondered what they thought when they received the Japanese postcard. In retrospect I can see it was cruel, but as a child I thought it was great. I guess I still really think it was kind of funny.

There must be few things more satisfying than seeing your children have teenagers of their own.

I'm glad I wasn't the one deciding the punishment for me. I would have said, "Grounded for this life and the next!"

There are many times when you will feel alone, but if you have family you will never feel lonely.

If you really want to find out what your children are thinking about you and show them how they are acting, try a role reversal day once a year.

Virginia Tech was a military school when I went through. Our freshman year was called our Rat Year. The upperclassmen had the right to treat us and abuse us mentally in any way they wished. And they did. For eight months all of us were subjected to the most extreme mental abuse you can think of. Some of the upperclassmen were well respected. Some were real jerks.

A few days before the end of the school year, a day was designated as Rat Day. This was the day freshmen were given all the privileges of upperclassmen and all upperclassmen had to behave like rats. On Rat Day, not only were freshmen allowed to hand out all the mental abuse they wished, but some physical abuse was allowed as well. Imagine how you would feel with a chance to finally get even with someone who had been your worst nightmare for the last eight months. Imagine how you would treat those who hadn't abused you, but who had helped you learn through discipline.

That was Rat Day. A day for the freshmen to be upperclassmen.

AND INTO THE TENT WE WENT

Carol and I tried this a couple of times with the kids. We were children for the day. (I don't like this food . . . I don't want to clean my room.)

The kids were allowed to be parents. (Eat everything on your plate . . . . Go clean your room right this minute.)

By the end of this role reversal day—Rat Day in the family—you will know exactly what your kids think of you. Believe it or not, your children will learn what you think of their behavior and how to handle leadership for the first time in their life.

ARE YOU GOING TO SCARBOROUGH FAIR?

Old people like to give good advice as solace for no longer being able to provide bad examples. Trying to get your children to do what you want them to do is like trying to herd a bunch of cats. The best way to give advice to your children is to find out what they want to do and advise them to do it.

TWO FACES HAVE I

I have a business life and a family life. Sometimes they are the same, and sometimes I act the same. More often than not, my family life is relaxed, and my business life is at a faster pace.

I DON'T CARE HOW MUCH MONEY I GOTTA SPEND

Every Thanksgiving or Christmas we always invite all of our children together, no matter where they are around the world. Even if it is just for a few hours. The renewed warmth is worth everything.

Tension can arise when you go home to visit your parents or they come to see you—they want to show they care and you want to show how you've grown. If everyone can agree to the following, affection replaces stress: When you are in my home, I'll take care of you. When I'm in your home, you take care of me.

All family together once a year—no matter what the cost.

EVERYTHING I WANT I HAVE

It is important for all of us to sit down and figure out who is really important in our lives. I suggest you take the top ten out of the eleven below, and after a long quiet walk on the beach, put them in order of importance to you. Here's who is important to me:

1. Family
2. God
3. Customers
4. Employees
5. Boss

6. Those who can't help themselves
7. Me
8. Those who have tried to screw me
9. Those who have screwed me
10. Those who can help themselves, but won't
11. Politicians, lawyers, and the press

THE BIG LESSONS

The most important things in the world aren't things. Use things and love people, not the other way around.

Treat your family as though they had only a day to live.

8 FRIENDS

Outside of my family, I really don't have many close friends. I have met some people I feel could be friends, but because everything is so fast these days, a real friend is something unusual. One friend in a lifetime is much; two are many; three are hardly possible.

My wife is my best friend. I'm assuming by the time this is published we are still married. We agree on everything, just not at the same time.

M . . . I . . . C . . . SEE YOU REAL SOON

A shadow is like most of those we call friends. Most friends are there only when the sun is shining. You will find out how few friends you really have when you lose your job, your fame, your power, or your money. Poof—they're gone.

JEREMIAH WAS A BULL FROG, HE WAS A . . .

Unfortunately it takes you a few years to find this out. I had been in the tennis business for about four years and was on the verge of bankruptcy. I was $50,000 overdrawn at the bank—extended as far as I thought I could be. I got a call from Harry. Harry was someone Carol and I had known professionally and personally for years. I liked him and trusted him. He attended the Air Force Academy and was one of the few not kicked out in a major cheating scandal. He was also a decorated fighter pilot in Nam. Our families got along well—in short, we were good friends.

Harry said he needed some money fast. I asked him how much. He said $60,000. I didn't have anything, but I told him to call back tomorrow and I'd see if there was anything I could do.

I went home and discussed it with Carol. She said to do whatever I thought was right. I went to our credit union and borrowed our limit—$5,000. That evening, even before I had talked to Harry, I sent him the check.

Harry and I talked briefly the next day. I told him $5,000 was all I could get and it was on its way. I never asked him what the money was for, never asked him for an IOU, but did tell him the credit union said I had to pay it back plus interest in six months. He said fine.

SU PRISE, SU PRISE, SUUU PRISE

Five months and twenty days later I called Harry. His wife answered. Harry had run away with a stewardess five months ago and she had no idea where he was. Harry didn't call when the six-month time limit hit. No call—no money. I was in a real bind. Five thousand dollars may not seem like much, but at the time, with us on the verge of going under, it was a mountain.

HAPPY TRAILS TO YOU, UNTIL WE MEET AGAIN

As a postscript, five years later I located Harry. It took me another full year to get the $5,000 back. No interest.

WE'LL SING IN THE SUNSHINE, WE'LL LAUGH EV'RY DAY

Even though you probably won't have many friends, you will still have a ton of acquaintances.

THE BIG LESSONS

Associate with people who will make you a better person.

He who laughs . . . lasts. Even better if they are honest.

Brian has always had a good sense of humor, even under pressure. When he was twelve, his appendix burst and we had to rush him to the hospital. As he was about to be operated on, he asked the doctor, "Will I be able to play the piano after this operation?" The doctor replied, "Of course." Brian shot back, "That's great, because I can't play it now." An old joke, but his timing would have pleased Groucho.

Spend time with those who have a positive attitude and a sense of humor.

I had just been elected to a very prestigious international board of directors. At dinner that night I proudly told the family, and my ego came out when I said, "I wonder how many great people there are in this industry." Brian, at that time age fourteen, didn't miss a bite of his burger as he said, "One less than you think."

9 VISION

Every once in a while, you will meet a person who can see years ahead with a telescope but can't get anyone to believe he has one. Vision is the art of seeing the invisible.

DO YOU SEE WHAT I SEE?

If you don't have a vision of where you're going, any road will take you there.

Vision creates a dream. Dreams become reality.

Alice: "Would you tell me, please, which way I ought to go from here?"
Cheshire: "That depends a good deal on where you want to get to."
Alice: "I don't much care where—"
Cheshire: "Then it doesn't matter which way you go."

FOR YOUR EYES ONLY

Everyone can have a vision of the future. The more specific the vision, the more you repeat the vision, the more the vision becomes part of your life, the more likely it is that it will occur. This is true in life, business, athletics—everything. We tend to get what we expect.

Tim and Tom Gullikson are twin brothers who played on the professional tennis tour. I recall Tom sitting at my club some years ago telling me he had a vision of being in the finals of Wimbledon with Tim. Tom's wife was on the couch sewing his shorts. They had just been on the tour a year or two and weren't making enough money even to buy tennis clothes.

Several years later I was watching the doubles finals at Wimbledon. One team was composed of John McEnroe and Peter Fleming—and the other team was Tom and Tim. Tom and Tim lost, which probably wasn't the exact vision Tom had in mind, but I thought it amazing. Even more astounding was, a few years later, Tom playing Tim in the men's senior finals at Wimbledon—Tom's vision was fulfilled.

You have the power in your hands if you have it in your mind.

YOU'RE THE ONE

The first day of every semester I ask my students to list their heroes. Their heroes are dramatically different from mine. My personal list is:

> **I believe I can predict the kind of society we will have in twenty years by seeing who the students' heroes are today.**

1. Jesus.
2. Wife. One of the students who went with me to Europe for a month said Carol had better be on the top of my list, since anyone who could put up with me for thirty-five years has to be a hero.
3. Leno. Here's one guy who really seems like he hasn't let fame change him. If he lost it all, he'd still have a good time.

> **The more the vision becomes part of your life, the more likely it will occur.**

4. Patton. Positive attitude, integrity, and results.
5. Parts of my children. One is an adventurer, one has a great sense of humor, one is very independent, and one has extreme inner confidence—all qualities I admire.

THE BIG LESSON

Decide what you will become. Your vision of the future will then become real. Imagination is even more valuable than knowledge.

> **Every day, visualize being what you want to be until it becomes part of your personality.**

10 SUCCESS

Being successful depends on your definition of success. There is always room at the top. If your definition includes money, fame, or power, you're going to find, although there are many paths to the top of the mountain, the view is always the same.

The mountaintop is an empty bag.

This is something you don't believe until you've been there. After you have achieved victory, you realize it was the trip that was enjoyable, not the destination. A celebrity is a person who works hard all his life to become well known, then wears dark glasses to avoid being recognized. It's the same for everyone.

I'LL TAKE WORK FOR FIVE HUNDRED, ALEX

Goal starts with go.

If you are going to climb the ladder, you must begin at the bottom. With much consistent effort, you will have much prosperity. You might give out, but never give up. The only person who ever got his work done by Friday was Robinson Crusoe. The slogan "press on" has solved and will always solve problems. Failure is no longer trying.

The dictionary is the only place where success comes before work.

There are a lot of people who have the will to win. What makes success is something that very few have—the will to prepare to win. Champions are not born, they are made.

The chains of habit are generally too small to be felt until they are too strong to be broken. Practice does not make perfect. Perfect practice makes perfect.

The difference between ordinary and extraordinary is just that little extra. Sometimes the difference between failure and success is doing a thing nearly right and doing a thing exactly right. Other times, it just depends on how well you can adjust to plan B.

IF YOU LIKE PEANUTS, YOU'LL LOVE SKIPPY

Simple plans work.

I've never faced a problem that couldn't be boiled down to a few important variables. True, a lot of other things might come into play, but focusing on one or two things will take care of most of the problem. The simpler things are, the better.

Whenever someone tells me the issue is complex or complicated, I know I'm in for a pile of BS.

BOND, JAMES BOND

Ready, fire, aim.

Wrong! The more exact the target, the more likely you will hit it. When you set an objective, it should be specific, quantifiable, and have a target date. If it can be done at any time, it will be done at no time. Deadlines are important.

Roman soldiers would not tie up their prisoners overnight. They would draw a line in the sand and instruct the prisoners to be there the next morning. Anyone not on the line at first light was hunted down and executed . . . a dead line.

ONE OF EVERY FIVE WHO TRY COCAINE GET HOOKED

Some people, when they miss a target, just change the target.

A BUMPER-TO-BUMPER WARRANTY

Not failure, but low aim is a crime.

Everything looks impossible for the people who never try anything. Anyone can be successful if they lie on the ground. Set your objectives as though you knew you could not fail, then figure out what you have to do to make them happen. You'll never know what you can do unless you try.

WARP 7, MR. SULU

Nothing is ever attempted if all possible objections must first be overcome.

One of the fallacies of university thinking is to teach you to study a problem to death. In business you don't have the time, staff, or financial resources to get all the information.

A good plan violently executed today is far better than a perfect plan executed next week.

He who hesitates is last.

Success begins when you overcome the fear of being unsuccessful. You can't hit a home run if you are afraid of striking out. Babe Ruth whiffed 1,330 times. Success is a marathon, not a sprint.

BOTH A DEVIL'S ADVOCATE AND A GOD'S ADVOCATE

Sometimes business goes well and sometimes it doesn't. The time to repair the roof is when the sun is shining.

When it is raining and a problem arises, first list facts and assumptions, then take the time to define the problem clearly. A problem well defined is half solved. Consider alternatives. The first possible solution should always be to do nothing. Then list your other alternatives with the pros and cons of each. Once you've picked a potential solution, make sure you have plan B to fall back on. Before taking action, consider what will happen if you are wrong.

Always focus on fixing the problem, never the blame.

STANDING ALL ALONE

The scenery only changes for the lead dog.

I'd much rather be first in a small village in Gaul than second in command in Rome.

There are three ways to do things here. The right way, the wrong way, and my way. It's my way or the highway.

I DECIDED LONG AGO NEVER TO LIVE IN ANYONE'S SHADOW

You'll never know who is right, but you will always know who is in charge. Once when the kids were in their teens and dinner was about to be served, there was a discussion about what we were going to do on the weekend. I carefully explained to our four children there were six votes in this family. I had one and Carol had five.

Before you command, you must learn to obey.

You really only know what it's like to carry the machine gun if you've done it. The best company president does not come out of Harvard Business School. He or she comes from the sales force or the production line.

SUPERMAN AND GREEN LANTERN AIN'T GOT NOTHING ON CAESAR

Before Caesar would take his troops into battle, he would put on a bright red cape in order to provide the enemy with a target.

Patton loved Caesar. Patton painted his tank bright red before a tank battle. The best leaders are always on the front line with a red cape on.

WHAT A WONDERFUL WORLD IT WILL BE

Better not successful with honor than successful by cheating.

THE BIG LESSON

If A equals success, then the formula is:
A = X + Y + Z
Where:

X is work
Y is play
Z is keep your mouth shut.

11
MONEY

What would you do if you lost all your property? Money really matters only when you don't have any. Once you have some, it loses its importance. Those people who think money will make you happy don't have money.

GIRL, THERE'S A BETTER LIFE FOR ME AND YOU

I can remember well those first years I was married. I was going to school and Carol was working. We had an income of less than $6,000 a year. Now our income is in six figures, but we don't live much differently now than we did then. As incredible as it sounds, during our first few years we considered Kool Aid a luxury.

A BRAND-NEW CRISP . . . SNAP! . . . SNAP! . . . $50 BILL

We didn't consider ourselves poor with $6,000 a year, and a good percentage went for books and tuition. Believe it or not, we didn't perceive we were "going without." Sure, it's easy to say money isn't important when you have some, but our standard of living hasn't changed much in three decades.

YOU CAN REPLACE LOST MONEY; YOU CAN'T REPLACE LOST TIME

Life is nothing but a cash flow. It is nice to build up a net worth, but your balance sheet only counts when you die.

THE BANK OF DAD

I hope my kids have been taught how to provide for themselves. If so, then I won't feel bad if my wife and I spend everything we have before we die.

MARRY MONEY

I also hope my children are not too money hungry. The best way to a man's wallet is to marry his daughter. And all heiresses are beautiful. But marrying someone you can get along with is better than marrying someone with deep pockets.

The best thing would be to find someone you can get along with who just happens to be rich.

THE BIG LESSON

Find something you love to do and you'll never have to work a day in your life. At least, you won't regard what you do as work. You will become prominent at what you do because it is fun. One day you'll turn around and find you have more success than you thought possible, and more money than you can spend.

12 BUSINESS

To understand business, you don't have to know much more than you do in chess. Unfortunately, you can't see all the pieces, not even your own. The pieces can move in ways that "aren't in the rules," and someone can knock over the board at any time.

Business is nothing more than a giant chess game.

THE PIECES

You've seen those balloons that have a balloon within a balloon. Pretend you have one, and the inside balloon represents your customer. When you start off a business, it is fairly easy to see through from the outside—you have a good idea of who the customer is, what they want, and what it will take to keep them happy.

The outside balloon looks like a beach ball. It has six sections. These sections represent the specific areas you can control—your product, price, location, promotion, staff, and finances.

As your business grows, the sizes of the balloons grow. The outside balloon becomes bigger and more difficult to see through. The inside balloon gets larger or may start to divide into smaller balloons.

You still have an idea what the customer looks like, but it is not nearly as clear as it used to be. The outside balloon continues to grow—so hefty you can barely hold it with your arms wrapped around it, so bulky you can no longer see all the sections.

An opportunity arises. You push one of the sections with one hand, only to find another section pops out. You increase the quality of the product to find the price has to go up. You increase the price and discover the number of sales go down. You decrease the staff to accommodate the reduction in sales, and with less staff the customer satisfaction goes down—and on and on and on.

So, business is nothing more than understanding that the outside balloon has six sections that we can manipulate in order to take care of the inside balloon—the customer.

MORE

You look down and you aren't quite standing on firm footing. You look all around and find you are in one of those "moon walk" air-jumping enclosures kids go into at carnivals.

As you are holding the balloons, almost more than you can control because they have gotten so big, you see several bullies entering the jumping room with you.

You try to talk to them. Two or three talk back to you. You think maybe one will be your friend and the friend will help you control your balloons. Most of the thugs pretend you don't exist.

They are all wired and start jumping. Before long, they are fighting among themselves. When the elephants fight the ants get smushed. You feel like an ant.

Who are these predators? They are all those things you can't control that have a tremendous effect on you and your business—the government, competition, taxes, economy, technology, weather, social changes, and cultural values.

At any time, one can destroy you and everything you have worked for. The only way you can survive is to understand what their favorite moves are and get out of their way.

All the time you are trying to stay out of the way, your balloons are getting bigger and bigger—you can't see the customer balloon any more—and the one thug you thought was your friend now turns on you.

Now you understand what business is.

MANAGEMENT'S VALUES

Find a company that has values similar to yours. If you believe in the same things their management believes in, you will prosper.

The best way to appreciate any job you have is to imagine yourself without one.

GOING INTO BUSINESS FOR YOURSELF?

Many students tell me they want to eventually own their own business. Here's what you need to understand to run a successful business.

Customers

Treat every customer as if he was a guest in your home and as if he was the only one in the world who paid your salary.

"Salary" comes from the Latin word for salt. Roman soldiers were paid in salt. Salt—salary.

Find out what your customers expect and consistently give them better attention, responsiveness, assurance, and empathy than they ever thought they'd get.

Marketing

Satisfying your customers' needs at a profit.

Price

The least you can charge is your cost. The most you can charge is the amount at which no one keeps buying. You will never know how high the upper limit is until you raise your price. Always find the roof.

Price yourself high. High prices give you enough leeway to service the customer well. Low prices, or giving it away, will make people think it is worth nothing. Low prices also mean that you cannot afford to service a customer.

If someone pays a lot, they will value their purchase dearly.

You can always lower your price if it's too high; it's tough to raise it if it's too low.

Product

Top shelf, no dust.

Make excellence your trademark. It is tough to go bankrupt if you are the very best. It is just as true for a product, a business, or an individual. Quality and excellence are your security.

How do you attain excellence and quality? By taking pride and joy in your work and making a conscious effort to improve every day. If you're not getting better, you're getting worse.

Quality is when your customers come back and your products don't.

Place

There are three important things in a retail business. Location, location, and location.

The reason Washington got stuck in Valley Forge was not because of lack of food—it was because his army ran out of shoes. Imagine how much business a cobbler would have had if he lived at Valley Forge.

Offshore

The hidden costs of laws and regulations, plus the obvious cost of required taxes, are escalating and are pushing us "out of business." In order to manufacture in the United States, you will have to meet one of these criteria:

You won't be able to afford to manufacture anything in the United States much longer.

1. You have a monopoly.
2. Bring out new products so fast that, effectively, you have a temporary monopoly.

3. Your manufacturing facilities have been paid for out of past profits or you bought your facilities from someone who had to take a hit.

In other words, the only way you will be able to manufacture anything in America will be if you have an unusual advantage. The run-of-the-mill facilities will not be located in the United States.

Nonretail service businesses will also move. The only thing keeping them here now is momentum. Why should the stock exchange be located in New York as opposed to the Caribbean?

The faces of New York remind me of a people who played a game and lost.

Retail service businesses will obviously remain here, but the cost per employee will rise so much that robots and computers will do much of the service.

When the minimum wage went up a few years ago, it became economical for the grocery business to put in bar code readers at the checkout line. The result was nine less employees in every grocery store.

Promotion

Find out from your customers what the most persuasive promise you can make to them is. Make sure you can deliver it, and then make it.

Advertising

Half of every dollar you spend will be wasted. You'll never know which half it is.

Positioning

Position yourself and your product next to quality. You will have more sales, at higher prices, than with any other alternative.

Perception

How would you like to be in charge of tourism for Iceland? Most people think Iceland is a cold, barren region. When the Vikings were out discovering land, they found an infertile, dull area. They also found a beautiful, picturesque land. But they wanted to keep the nice place for themselves, so they pulled the first great branding move. They called the armpit terrain "Greenland" and the exquisite region "Iceland." Hundreds of years later people still think Greenland is beautiful and Iceland is sterile.

When perception is different from reality, it is the perception you must deal with.

The only person who likes change is a wet baby. It is an opportunity you can guide but not control. The key words to remember when dealing with change are "anticipate," "adapt," "act."

Management

Or, getting someone else to do all the work.

While I was in the army in Europe, I got my masters in business. It was an experimental program where we flew the profs from the University of Utah to Germany. There were only five students in the class, and one was a Colonel Blass. He was always calling me up to help him with his homework. I was a captain, and whenever he called I would politely tell him I had work to do. I couldn't get away to help him with his homework.

Judging from the number of phone calls I received, it was obvious Colonel Blass had lots of time to study—and took it. One day we had an unusually difficult homework problem involving some sophisticated statistical analysis with calculus—pretty deep. I had a heavy math background, so it was not difficult for me. He knew that.

The colonel called me at one P.M. He said he needed help with the problem. I told him I was in the middle of preparing a briefing for the general and couldn't leave. He then said, "Captain, this is a colonel. You have ten minutes to get into my office." When I am ordered to do something, I do it.

His office was immaculate.

The only things on his huge desk were his homework and a two-tiered in-box. The top of the box said "Colonel Blass." The bottom said "Devereux for action." Once you achieve a high rank in the military, it is common to have a civilian assistant. Mr. Devereux was the colonel's assistant. I had never been in the colonel's office before, and I knew he was in charge of some very important things. But he never seemed to work on those things—just his homework.

He sat behind his desk and I sat down in front of it. We started working on the problem. About ten minutes later, his secretary rushed in the room with a stack of top secret documents and said, "The general wants an answer to this within the hour." The Colonel didn't even look up. "Put it in my box."

I then discovered why he had so much time to do homework. As she put the papers in his box, they fell straight through to Devereux's. The colonel had removed the bottom part of his box that would have held papers for him. Colonel Blass—Master Delegator.

DAILY OPERATIONS

It's just like the game at the carnival—"whack the mole." You take a mallet and hit a mole as it

Speed saves money and satisfies customers.

pops up. You hit that mole and another leaps up. As fast as you can move, moles pop up and you swat at them. Sometimes you hit the mole (a problem solved), and sometimes you miss it.

Hit the moles as fast as you can. The speed of the leader determines the speed of the pack.

OBJECTIVES

Expect and inspect.

You will always have satisfactory results just by measuring what is going on. What gets measured gets done.

If you want to have good results, measure your people against each other and publicize who achieved what.

If you want to have great results, allow your people to establish their own objectives, broadcast them, and then measure and publicize the results.

CORPORATE CULTURE

Your company's success will be directly related to how well you communicate your dream and get your people to participate in it.

Corporate culture is a disease every one of your employees will catch. But the culture is yours to determine.

THE VISION

Your job is not to establish the intermediate and day-to-day objectives. Let your people do that. Steer the boat, don't row it. Your job is to get everyone to understand your values and to share in your vision of where you are going.

Seeing the big picture is essential. If the owners of the railroads had understood they were in the transportation business (they thought they were in the railroad business), they would have controlled air travel!

THE ORGANIZATION CHART

Put yourself on top, your management staff below, the workers below them, and then the customers at the bottom. This is the "traditional" pyramid form of organization.

Then turn the organization chart upside down.

The ones on the top will be the customers, the ones next to the top will be those in direct contact with the customers, and so on. You will be on the bottom. This chart will now show everyone, including you, who is really important to the success of the company.

You will be pleasantly surprised how much your business can accomplish if you allow your people to get the credit.

WHO TO HIRE

The three-legged stool! Find me those with a great attitude (you can't teach someone to be nice), unquestioned integrity, and a track record of results.

THE BIG CHALLENGE

Enormous problems are built up one small failure at a time, but they can be solved by one small success at a time.

Sloppiness always costs money.

The more haste the less speed.

I don't remember where I read this, but I recall that Henry Ford took the person who was doing an impeccable job of sweeping up the factory and made him his chief metallurgical engineer. The point is, if you can find that rare individual who does small things right, you can safely assume they will do big things right. If you have to make a choice between speed and doing a job right, take the time to do it right. Some people forget how fast you did a job, but everyone remembers how well you did it. No one hates a job well done.

It takes less time to do a thing right than to explain why you did it wrong.

HOW MANY TO HIRE

More with less.

If your people have time to complain, they don't have enough to do. Figure out how many people you need to do the job and then hire 75 percent of that amount. Good people always like more work than they can handle—it makes the day go faster and is much more interesting.

Better to understaff at the start than to use the Mongolian horde approach.

Fewer people force a simple organization chart and chain of command. In addition to the obvious savings, you will achieve crisp decisions and clear accountability for those decisions.

WHO HIRES

Let your best person do the hiring. First-class people hire first-class people. Second-class people hire third-class people.

Once you have a first-class team (notice there is no I in team), let your best person select the final candidates. Then allow the people they will be working with to make the final hire. The way you develop teamwork is to give the team work.

Results will eventually come for those who have the right attitude and integrity. For those who don't, it doesn't matter what kind of results they produce—eliminate them. And get rid of anyone who is constantly fighting you or the corporation. Their attitude won't improve.

LABOR RELATIONS

If you treat your employees as though they are as important as they really are, a strike should never happen. If it does, they have the right to not work. But you have the right to go about your business and hire permanent replacements or close the doors for good.

Employees don't really care how much you know until they know how much you really care.

COMPENSATION

An adequate base so they know they won't starve. A small menu of benefits. They choose from the menu—you pay a percentage (say 50 percent, and they pay 50 percent) and the menu has a dollar cap.

The more employees act like owners or entrepreneurs, the better.

Add high incentives, immediate rewards. Bag anything long-term.

JOB DESCRIPTIONS

Most are filled with activities. The best spell out the decisions the person is expected to make and the results they are expected to obtain.

All the textbooks say hire the person to fit the job description. No. If you find a great person, hire him or her. Then find something they would love to do.

SALES

Every potential customer asks three questions:

1. Can I trust you?
2. Are you committed to excellence?
3. Do you really care about me?

As long as the answer is yes, you will always have all the sales you need.

Kindness is the only language the blind can see and the deaf can hear.

COMPETITION

Those who say competition is a good thing don't have any. Competition should either be acquired or destroyed.

MARKET SHARE

Once you have established a track record and have built up a wallet, you can afford to gain market share, even if you have to sell to some customers at a low price. There is a definite correlation between high market share and long-term profitability. Every customer you have is one your competitors don't.

Once you control the market, then you control prices.

FINANCES

Cash flow is the name of the game.

Expenses

Pick out your three biggest expenses and concentrate all of your cost control efforts on them. Always spend more than you think prudent on promotion.

Spending

Spending expands to consume the cash available.

Spend whatever it takes to thoroughly understand your customers and competitors. Unless any other proposed spending will result in long-term customer satisfaction or repeat business, don't spend the money.

Investing

Buy the best you can with what you've got and take a risk. This is not just putting all your eggs in one basket—it is getting the one best egg you can afford.

Accounting

For management: Knowing what the real revenues and expenses are.

For stockholders: Making sure revenues exceed expenses.

For the IRS: Making sure expenses exceed revenues.

Profit

With profit you can do everything; without it nothing.

Taxes

Don't mess with the IRS. Pay them.

There is a difference between the tax collector and the taxidermist. The taxidermist leaves the hide.

Banks

Banks only want to lend you money when you don't need any. But it is their money, so that's their decision. I'd like the same repayment plan as Brazil.

Debt to equity ratio: More equity, less debt.

Raising equity

There are two times in a business life when it is easy to raise equity. One is obviously when you have been in business for some time and have a solid track record. The other time, and this one is often overlooked, is when the business is nothing but an idea.

STOCKHOLDERS

Unless you own 100 percent of the company, it is your obligation to make every decision in the best interests of the owners and customers, never for your own benefit.

STARTING YOUR FIRST BUSINESS

Expenses will be twice your projections; revenues half.

GETTING ASSISTANCE

The power sentence: "I've got a problem and I need your help."

NEGOTIATION

You are going to run into a lot of people who, in a fifty-fifty deal, still want to get the hyphen. I don't like to bargain, unless we both feel like we are benefiting.

When I make an offer, my first offer is always my best. I'd rather not do business with someone who likes to squeeze.

But if I have to, and they do start to push, I withdraw my first offer and my next offer is not as good as my first. The more the other person presses, the less they get. I've lost out on some deals this way, but I also got to do business on my terms with many who were only out for themselves.

You may have to do business again with this person, so it doesn't pay to grab everything for yourself. Don't squeeze the lemons dry. Leave some juice for others.

To be a confident negotiator you need preparation and experience. If you don't have much experience, then overcompensate with preparation.

ETHICS

The gap between what we know is right and what we do. When in doubt, do what's right.

I went to school in South Philadelphia for grades six through eight. It was tough—zip guns, knives, and gangs.

But, even at twelve, it was obvious to me who was going to make it out. It was the kids whose parents took control of them—the ones who were not allowed out at night to play, were forced to wear nice clothes and study. I know now if your parents made you work, learn, and behave, you can make it out. I didn't fully understand it then, but I was learning early the advantages of having caring, concerned, and noncompromising parents.

Your parents grew up believing they would take care of you when you were young and you would take care of them when they got old. As the government has become the parent for the child and the child for the parent, business has pulled back from voluntarily providing for the community.

Your social obligation is inversely proportional to the amount of government programs. If the future brings fewer government services, your duty will be to provide more.

HERE'S A STORY, ABOUT A LADY

Carol provides balance. She gives her time and donates at least 10 percent of our gross to several charities. (She believes we all gain when we give.) Plus, the Feds grab 25 percent; the State gets 15 percent; and we all pay at least 30 percent in the form of higher prices caused by regulations and hidden taxes. . . . Hmmmmm. Once I add up all those percentages, I can see why our standard of living hasn't changed in thirty years.

The more things change, the more things stay the same.

THE BIG LESSON

Business is simple. All you have to remember is to make sure your revenues exceed expenses. P.S. It may be simple. But it is not easy.

CONCLUSION

So what?

AND I KNOW THAT MY SONG ISN'T SAYING ANYTHING NEW

What in this book is so profound? Maybe not much. But if you have found some things that allow you to make better decisions, live a happier life, or be more successful, then it has been worth your time to read and my time to write.

RESEARCHERS CAUSE CANCER IN RATS

You may have noticed a sprinkling of trivia throughout the book.

Trivia—from two Latin words meaning "three roads." What, you ask, do three roads have to do with trivia? Three men used to meet to exchange stories. They all had to walk down a different path. They met and exchanged their stories in a fork in the road—where the three roads met.

I added trivia if I thought it was interesting or helped illustrate a point.

This was not meant to be an attempt at a philosophical set of memoirs. Rather, this is meant to be the collection of arrows in my belief quiver.

When you put down the good things you ought to have done, and leave out the bad things you did—that's called memoirs.

EXIT STAGE LEFT

I was asked what I consider to be the most important principles. Here are my two—make that three—tablets:

1. Family, God, and honor are far more important than money, fame, or power.
2. I complained because I had no shoes until I met a man who had no feet.
3. Treat your family as if they were going to die tomorrow.
4. You are what you believe you are. You become what you believe you will become.
5. You can learn all you need to about a person if you play some games with them and see what they laugh at.

6. Don't eat the yellow snow.
7. Kindness is the only language the blind can see and the deaf can hear.
8. Take the golden rule platinum.
9. Find something you love and you'll never have to work a day the rest of your life.
10. Treat your body as if it were the only one you'll ever have.
11. In the land of the blind, the one-eyed man is king.
12. Hang on to sixteen as long as you can.
13. Opportunity is like Chickenman.
14. Put your red cape on.
15. When you get ready to die, make sure you don't turn around and say you haven't lived.

SAY GOOD NIGHT, GRACIE

I realize the only thing that will determine the size of my funeral is the weather. I will not be remembered for what I did. I might be remembered for what my children thought I did.

APPENDIX A

COLOR HIM FATHER, COLOR HIM LOVE

When I was . . .

3 years old.	I can't wait to see Daddy when he comes home.
5 years old.	My Daddy knows everything.
10 years old.	How come dad didn't know that?
13 years old.	He just doesn't understand what it's like to be a kid today.
16 years old.	I don't want to be near dad.
19 years old.	If there is anyone who doesn't have a clue, it is dad.
21 years old.	No one I know can relate to dad.
26 years old.	Dad might know something about it, but that's only because he's so old.
36 years old.	I've got to call Dad to see what I should do.
46 years old.	It would have been good to know what Dad would have done.
56 years old.	He knew everything. I would give anything just to see Dad one more time.

APPENDIX B

The following listing contains the sources for all lyrics mentioned on the pages given: 5—"This is dedicated to the one I love": "Dedicated to the One I Love," Mamas and Papas, 1967, by Lowman Pawling and R. Bass, 1967; "Get your motor running . . . ": "Born to Be Wild," Steppenwolf, 1968, by Mars Bonfire. 23—"Within the prison walls of my mind": "Over You," Gary Puckett and the Union Gap, 1968, words and music by J. Fuller; "Crimson and clover/Over and over": "Crimson and Clover," Tommy James and the Shondells, 1969, by Peter Lucia, Jr., and Tommy James, © 1968 Big Seven Music. 25—"I haven't got time for the pain": "Haven't Got Time for the Pain," Carly Simon, 1974, by Carly Simon and Jacob Brackman. 28—"You got to know when to hold 'em": "The Gambler," Kenny Rogers, 1978, by Don Schlitz, © 1978 Writers Night Music; "Take this job and love it": "Take This Job and Shove It," Johnny Paycheck, by

David Allan Coe, © 1977 Warner-Tamerlane. 29—"Everything I want I have": "This Magic Moment," Jay and the Americans, 1969, words and music by Doc Pomus and Mort Shuman, © 1960 Rumbalero Music; "You don't know what you've got until you lose it": "You Don't Know," Ral Donner, 1961, by Mike Hawker and John Schroeder; "He ain't heavy": "He Ain't Heavy, He's My Brother," the Hollies, 1970, words by Bob Russell, music by Bobby Scott, © 1969 Harrison Music/Jenny Music. 30—"Celebrate, celebrate, dance to the music": "Celebrate," Three Dog Night, 1970, words and music by Alan Gordon and Garry Bonner, © 1968 Alley Music Corp. and Trio Music/All rights administered by Hudson Bay Music; "Skyrockets in flight": "Afternoon Delight," Starland Vocal Band, 1976, words and music by Bill Danoff, © Cherry Lane Music; "Raindrops on roses and whiskers on kittens": "My Favorite Things," from *The Sound of Music,* words and music by Oscar Hammerstein II and Richard Rodgers, © 1959 by Richard Rodgers and Oscar Hammerstein. 32—"Ninety miles an hour down a dead end road": "Small Town Saturday Night," Hank Ketchum, 1991. 33—"You can't please everyone, so you've got to please yourself": "Garden Party," Rick Nelson, 1972, © 1972 Matragun Music. 34—"Gonna make it happen": "Born to Be Wild," Steppenwolf, 1968, by Mars Bonfire; "Ain't no mountain high enough": "Ain't No Mountain High

Enough," Diana Ross, 1970, by Nickolas Ashford and Valerie Simpson, © 1967 Jobete Music. 35—"Creatures keep on creatching": "Higher Ground," Stevie Wonder, 1973, words and music by Stevie Wonder, © 1973 Jobete Music and Black Bull Music; "Another page of history turned and the beat goes on": "The Beat Goes On," Sonny and Cher, 1967, words and music by Sonny Bono, © 1967 Cotillion Music and Chris-Marc Music. 36—"Lucy must know that the world is flat 'cause when someone leaves town they never come back": "Small Town Saturday Night," Hank Ketchum, 1991. 37—"Oz never did give anything to the tin man that he didn't already have": "Tin Man," America, 1974, words and music by Dewey Bunnell, © 1974 WB Music. 38—"Don't know what a slide rule is for": "Wonderful World," Sam Cooke, 1960, words and music by Sam Cooke, Herb Alpert, and Lou Adler, © 1959 Kags Music. 39—"Heard it through the grapevine": "I Heard It Through the Grapevine," Marvin Gaye, 1968, by Norman Whitfield and Barrett Strong, © 1967 Jobete Music. 40—"Studying hard, hoping to pass": "School Day," Chuck Berry, 1957, words and music by Chuck Berry, © 1957 Arc Music. 41—"I think you'll understand": "I Want to Hold Your Hand," the Beatles, 1964, words and music by John Lennon and Paul McCartney, © 1963 Northern Songs Ltd. 44—"As I walk along I wonder what went wrong": "Runaway," Del Shannon, 1961, words and music by Del Shannon and Max Crook, © 1961 Mole Hole Music and Noma Music, administered by Bug Music Group. 47—"Doe, a deer, a female deer": "Do-Re-Mi," from *The Sound of Music,* words and music by Oscar Hammerstein II and Richard Rodgers, © 1959 by Richard Rodgers and Oscar Hammerstein. 50—"I ran all the way home": "Sorry (I Ran All the Way Home)," The Impalas, 1959, words and music by Harry Giosasi and Artie Zwirn, © 1957 Big Seven Music. 51—"Poetry in motion, dancing close to me": "Poetry in Motion," Johnny Tillotson, 1960, by Paul Kaufman and Mike Anthony, © 1960 Meridian Music, assigned to Vogue Music. 52—"You know it don't come easy": "It Don't Come Easy," Ringo Starr, 1971, by Richard Starkey. 53—"Billie Joe never had a lick of sense, pass the biscuits, please": "Ode to Billie Joe," Bobbie Gentry, 1967, words and music by Bobbie Gentry; "I touch no one and no one touches me": "I Am a Rock," Simon and Garfunkel, 1966, words and music by Paul Simon, © 1965 Paul Simon. 54—"In the desert you can't remember your name": "A Horse with No Name," America, 1972, words and music by Dewey Bunnell, © 1971 Warner Bros. Music. 56—"Teacher is teaching the golden rule": "School Day," Chuck Berry, 1957, words and music by Chuck Berry, © 1957 Arc Music. 57—"You keep lying when you should be truthin'": "These Boots Are Made for Walkin'," Nancy Sinatra,

1966, by Lee Hazelwood, © 1965 Criterion Music. 58—"I feel good, I knew that I would": "I Got You (I Feel Good)," words and music by James Brown, © 1966 Lois Publishing and Try Me Music. 59—"I bet you're wondrin' how I knew": "I Heard It Through the Grapevine," Marvin Gaye, 1968, by Norman Whitfield and Barrett Strong, © 1967 Jobete Music. 61—"We may never pass this way again": "We May Never Pass This Way (Again)," Seals and Crofts, 1973, words and music by James Seals and Dash Crofts, © 1973 Dawnbreaker Music. 62—"Devil with a blue dress on": "Devil with a Blue Dress," Mitch Ryder, 1966, words and music by William Stevenson and Frederick Long, © 1964 Jobete Music; "Knock knock knockin' on heaven's door": "Knockin' on Heaven's Door," Bob Dylan, 1973, by Bob Dylan, © 1973 Ram's Horn Music. 64—"How can I be sure, in a world that's constantly changing?": "How Can I Be Sure," the Rascals, 1967, by Felix Cavaliere and Edward Brigati, Jr., © 1967 Coral Music and Downtown Music. 66—"Don't be concerned./It will not harm you./It's only me pursuing something I'm not sure of": "Elusive Butterfly," Bob Lind, 1966, by Bob Lind, © 1965 Unart Music and Metric Music. 67—"Though it's always crowded, you still can find some room": "Heartbreak Hotel," Elvis Presley, 1956, by Elvis Presley, Mae Boren Axton, and Tommy Durden, © 1956 Tree Publishing; "I believe for every drop of rain that falls": "I

Believe," words and music by Ervin Drake, Irvin Graham, Jimmy Shirl, and Al Stillman, © 1952 Hampshire House Publishing. 69—"Give me just a little more time": "Give Me Just a Little More Time," Chairmen of the Board, 1970, by R. Dunbar and E. Wayne. 70—"Time can do so much": "Unchained Melody," the Righteous Brothers, 1965, words by Hy Zaret, music by Alex North, © 1955 Frank Music. 71—"Tell the teacher we're surfin'": "Surfin' U.S.A.," the Beach Boys, 1963, words by Brian Wilson, music by Chuck Berry, © 1958 Arc Music; "Crying over you": "Crying," Roy Orbison, 1961, by Roy Orbison and Joe Nelson, © 1961 Acuff-Rose Publications. 72—"When the dog bites, when the bee stings": "My Favorite Things," from *The Sound of Music,* words and music by Oscar Hammerstein II and Richard Rodgers, © 1959 by Richard Rodgers and Oscar Hammerstein; "Bluer than blue": "Bluer Than Blue," Michael Johnson, 1978, words and music by Al Lewis, Larry Stock, and Vincent Rose, © 1940 Chappell & Co., copyrights assigned to Chappell & Co and Sovereign Music; "Gotta start a new life": "Take a Letter, Maria," R. B. Greaves, 1969, by R. B. Greaves. 73—"Oh! Carol": "Oh! Carol," Neil Sedaka, 1959, by Howard Greenfield and Neil Sedaka, © 1959 Screen Gems–EMI Music. 74—"The cat's in the cradle": "Cat's in the Cradle," Harry Chapin, 1974, by Harry and Sandy Chapin, © 1974

Story Songs Ltd.; "Turn around and you're two, turn around and you're four, turn around and you're a young girl going out of the door": "Turn Around," words and music by Malvina Reynolds, Allen Green, and Harry Belafonte, © 1958 Clara Music Publishing; "Ring ring goes the bell": "School Day," Chuck Berry, 1957, words and music by Chuck Berry, © 1957 Arc Music. 77—"Bright are the stars that shine,/Dark is the sky": "And I Love Her," the Beatles, 1964, by John Lennon and Paul McCartney, © 1964 Northern Songs Ltd. 78—"Put me in, coach, I'm ready to play. . . today": "Centerfield," John Fogerty, 1985, by J. C. Fogerty, © 1984 Wenaha Music; "Keep me searching for a heart of gold . . . and I'm getting old": "Heart of Gold," Neil Young, 1972, words and music by Neil Young, © 1971 Silver Fiddle. 79—"I can't wait forever, time won't let me": "Time Won't Let Me," the Outsiders, 1966, words by Chet Kelly, music by Tom King, © 1966 Beechwood Music. 80—"Stuck inside these four walls, trapped inside forever": "Band on the Run," Paul McCartney & Wings, words and music by Paul and Linda McCartney, © 1974 McCartney Music. 81—"Got on board a westbound 747": "It Never Rains in Southern California," Albert Hammond, 1972, words and music by Albert Hammond and Mike Hazelwood, © 1972 Landers-Roberts Music/rights administered by April Music. 82—"Hello Mudduh, hello Faddah. Here I am at . . . ": "Hello Mudduh, Hello Faddah," Allan Sherman, 1963, words and music by Allan Sherman. 83—"Wooly bully": "Wooly Bully," Sam the Sham and the Pharaohs, 1965, words and music by Domingo Samudio, © 1964 Beckie Publishing. 84—"And into the tent we went": "Ahab the Arab," Ray Stevens, 1962, words and music by Ray Stevens, © 1962 Lowery Music; "Are you going to Scarborough Fair?": "Scarborough Fair/Canticle," Simon and Garfunkel, 1966, words and music by Simon & Garfunkel/Arrangement and Original Counter Melody, © 1966 Paul Simon; "Two faces have I": "Two Faces Have I," Lou Christie, 1963, words and music by Lou Sacco and Twyla Herbert, © Painted Desert Music. 85—"I don't care how much money I gotta spend": "The Letter," the Box Tops, 1967, by Wayne Carson Thompson, © 1967 Earl Barton Music; "Everything I want I have": "This Magic Moment," Jay and the Americans, 1969, words and music by Doc Pomus and Mort Shuman, © 1960 Rumbalero Music. 88—"Jeremiah was a bull frog, he was a . . ." "Joy to the World," Three Dog Night, 1970, words and music by Hoyt Axton, © 1970 Lady Jane Music. 89—"Happy trails to you, until we meet again": "Happy Trails," Roy Rogers and Dale Evans; "We'll sing in the sunshine, we'll laugh ev'ry day": "We'll Sing in the Sunshine," Gale Garnett, 1964, words and music by Gale

Garnett, © 1963 Lupercalia Music Publishing. 92—"For your eyes only": "For Your Eyes Only," Sheena Easton, 1981, words by Michael Leeson, music by Bill Conti, © 1981 Danjaq USA, all rights controlled by United Artists Music and Unart Music, all rights assigned to CBS Catalogue Partnership; "You're the one": "You're the One," the Vogues, 1965. 99—"I decided long ago never to live in anyone's shadow": "The Greatest Love of All," Whitney Houston, 1991, words by Linda Creed, music by Michael Masser, © 1977 Golden Torch Music and Gold Horizon Music. 100—"What a wonderful world it will be": "Wonderful World," Sam Cooke, 1960, words and music by Sam Cooke, Herb Alpert, and Lou Adler, © 1959 Kags Music. 101—"Girl, there's a better life for me and you": "We Gotta Get Out of This Place," the Animals, 1965. 125—"Here's a story, about a lady": *The Brady Bunch*. 126—"And I know that my song isn't saying anything new": "After the Loving," Engelbert Humperdinck, 1977, by Alan Bernstein and Ritchie Adams, © 1974 Silver Pine Music and Oceans Blue. 129—"Color him father, color him love": "Color Him Father," the Winstons, 1969, by Richard Spencer.

So if you find a mistake or something that hasn't received proper credit, please let me know. I'll make the correction.

If you have some aphorisms that guide you in your

life, please write. I'll try to include them in future editions. Or if you would just like to tell me what you think of the book, my home address is:

Charley Swayne
N 1964 Crestview Place
La Crosse, Wisconsin 54601, U.S.A.

This was originally written as a graduation present for my students. If you are a former student and don't have a copy, please write. I'll send you a copy as my gift.

If one of your parents gave you this, they understand children will take advice from a stranger they wouldn't take from their own parents. You now know I have an opinion on everything, but that doesn't mean it's true. The real answers are not in this book, they are in you.

Elvis has left the building.

APPENDIX C

If you thought you recognized some of the thoughts in the book, you're right. Here's a list of all the "people"—real and otherwise—whose sentiments grace these pages.

PAGE	QUOTE	SOURCE
10	Why Didn't . . . Me That?	Book title suggested by Cory Rudd
10	A Student's . . . Real World)	Book title suggested by Jennifer Tyler
10	A Graduating . . . in College	Book title suggested by Mark McCasslin
10	Everything College . . . but Didn't	Book title suggested by Sue Kruncos
10	Real Life 101	Book title suggested by Michael Schulz
10	All the . . . Teach You	Book title suggested by Tammy Nicolai

10	What a . . . Is Over	Book title suggested by Kim Duffy and Matt McDevitt
10	Graduating Seniors . . . Should Have	Book title suggested by Kathy Davis
13	Viewer Mail	David Letterman, *Late Night with David Letterman*
13	Experience is . . . our mistakes.	Oscar Wilde, *Lady Windermere's Fan* (1892)
14	The older I . . . I know.	Charlie Brown, *Peanuts* comic strip
14	idealism increases . . . the problem.	John Galsworthy
14	Beavis	*Beavis and Butt-head,* TV program Mike Judge
14	I started . . . said before.	Terence, 160 B.C.
15	when you're . . . up speed.	Charlie Brown, *Peanuts* comic strip
16	When I . . . so sure.	Jean de La Bruyère, *Les Caractères. Des Ouvrages de l'Esprit* (1688)
18	Your whole . . . decision points.	Bud Fox, *Wall Street*
21	A visiting . . . back tomorrow.	Billy Packer

23	If you . . . you're right.	Virgil
23	Who do . . . great attitude?	Earl Nightingale
24	Survey says	Richard Dawson, host, *Family Feud*
24	treat it . . . amusement park.	*Laverne and Shirley*
25	He's 110 . . . over 100.	*Wizard of Id,* comic strip
25	For his . . . "the soup."	Terry Ferebee
26	you are . . . you eat	*You Are What You Eat,* Victor H. Lindlhr
26	Say kiiidds . . . is it?	Buffalo Bob, *Howdy Doody*
28	The only . . . use them.	Terry Ferebee
28	Every one . . . of time.	Jay Conrad Levinson
29	every horse . . . the heaviest?	Thomas Fuller, 1732
29	Charlene: All the bachelors	*Cathy,* comic strip
30	No one . . . bright side.	Terry Ferebee
30	I am . . . I am happy.	Alain-René Lesage, 1715
30	We never . . . runs dry.	Thomas Fuller, 1732
31	What do . . . kemo sabe?	Jay Silverheels (Tonto), *Lone Ranger*

31	You can . . . laugh at.	Johann Goethe, 1809
32	Anyone who is more than	Bernard Baruch
32	to accomplish . . . never die	Emile Littré, 1877
33	A journey . . . single step.	Lao-tzu, *The Way of Lao-tzu*
33	Nothing seems . . . we don't.	Maxim Gorki, 1903
33	If you . . . your attitude.	Brian Swayne
33	Chickennnn . . . mannnnn . . . he's everywhere	Radio character
34	The only . . . recognize it.	Ann Landers
35	The greatest . . . make one.	Elbert Hubbard, 1927
35	Failure is . . . than before.	Terry Ferebee
35	You get . . . get old.	George Burns
35	Most people . . . they die.	Oliver Wendell Holmes, 1860
35	On the . . . the edge.	O. B. Gray
37	It's amazing . . . be done.	*Garfield,* comic strip
37	To get . . . will become.	Earl Nightingale
38	We are . . . different things.	Will Rogers

38	When you . . . else knows.	Bob Fitzgerald
38	Having nothing . . . saying it.	Frank Tyger
38	We were . . . we talk.	Zeno of Citium, 300 B.C.
38	It is . . . the answers.	James Thurber, *Saying,* (1945)
39	It is . . . all doubt.	Will Rogers
39	You never . . . haven't said.	Terry Ferebee
39	We are . . . to dance.	Alan Harrington, 1959
39	They give . . . of others	Aesop
41	The fool . . . a fool.	Shakespeare, *As You Like It*
43	He explained . . . of students	Dan Gelatt, regent, University of Wisconsin, La Crosse
44	The new world order	Alice A. Bailey
44	I'll buy a vowel	*Wheel of Fortune*
45	Thoughts, like . . . bite everyone.	Jacek Galazka, 1962
46	The mark of the Z	*Zorro*
47	Knowledge comes . . . will lingers.	Alfred Lord Tennyson, *Locksley Hall* (1842)

48	The wisest people follow their own direction.	Euripides, 414 B.C.
48	wise people . . . the time.	Ralph Waldo Emerson, 1860
50	Tough times . . . people do.	Flip Saunders
50	If it . . . you stronger.	Joe Cirulli
50	The strongest . . . hottest fire.	Richard Nixon
51	In the . . . is king	Michael Qpostolius, 1400
51	Everything I . . . my own	Johann Goethe, 1774
52	You are . . . to do.	U.S. military
52	That's a . . . Mrs. Cleaver	Eddie Haskel, *Leave It to Beaver*
53	You may . . . the responsibility.	U.S. military
53	Initiative is . . . being told.	Victor Hugo
53	Underpromise and overdeliver.	Frank Uhler
54	Instead of . . . look good	John Sununu
54	You know . . . the floor?	Malay proverb
54	the cards . . . good hand?	Jonathan Swift, 1711

54	The price . . . is responsibility.	Winston Churchill
55	Your mission . . . accept it	*Mission: Impossible*
56	Moses came . . . ten commandments."	*History of the World, Part I*
57	It is always the strongest argument.	Sophocles, 435 B.C.
57	You don't . . . the truth	Mark Twain, 1910
57	you sure . . . to whom	Marcus Quintilian, *De Institutione Oratoria,* A.D. 95
57	Whatever will . . . out immediately.	Henry Kissinger
57	It fears no trial.	Thomas Fuller, 1732
60	When you . . . get fleas.	Victor Brick
61	Fool me . . . on me.	Thomas Fuller, 1732
61	There was . . . tried before.	Mae West, *Klondike Annie* (1936)
61	I could . . . except temptation.	Oscar Wilde, *Lady Windermere's Fan* (1892)
62	Now I . . . still evil.	Max Lerner, 1959
62	Two thumbs down	Siskel and Ebert, film critics
62	Everyone is a moon . . . to anybody.	Mark Twain, *Following the Equator* (1897)

62	awful acts . . . everyday occurrences.	Alexander Chase, 1966
62	When you . . . is watching?	H. L. Mencken, 1920
63	The shadow knows	*The Shadow,* radio program
64	When there . . . is conscience.	Publilius Syrus, 100 B.C.
64	Everyone's true . . . they compete.	Ovid, A.D. 8
64	If you . . . for anything.	Dennis Waitley
66	the universe . . . the earth?	*A Brief History of Time,* Stephen W. Hawking
67	The Supreme . . . during earthquakes	Jay Leno
67	Religion is . . . of morality.	William Bennett
68	Faith must . . . can't be.	Will Rogers
68	God will . . . full ones	Publilius Syrus, 100 B.C.
69	Life is . . . its speed.	Mohandas Gandhi
69	The day . . . back in.	Frank Bucaro
71	getting ready to live	Ralph Waldo Emerson, *Journals* (1834)
71	The F word . . . fun	Terry Ferebee
71	Those who . . . being wrong?	A & E Improv

71	Everything you . . . your eyes.	David Birney
72	The first . . . stop digging.	Senator Phil Gramm
74	Not every . . . a teacher.	William Bennett
76	Discipline builds inner confidence	*Leadership Secrets of Attila the Hun,* Wess Roberts
77	Neither your . . . are challenged.	Publilius Syrus, *Maxim* (100 B.C.)
77	There is . . . to fail.	Eric Hoffer, 1964
78	Childhood memories . . . long haul.	Kevin Arnold, *Wonder Years*
78	There is . . . of success	J. Paul Getty
78	When you win, nothing hurts.	Joe Namath
79	What we . . . to communicate.	*Cool Hand Luke*
80	It is . . . at all.	George Courtline, 1917
82	There must . . . their own.	Doug Larson
84	Old people like . . . bad examples.	François La Rochefoucauld, *Reflections* (1665)
84	Trying to . . . of cats.	Hillary Clinton
84	The best way . . . do it.	Harry Truman
84	I have . . . family life.	Ralph Waldo Emerson, 1860

85	All family . . . the cost.	Norman Vincent Peale
85	When you . . . of me.	Janice Thorn
86	The most . . . aren't things.	Terry Ferebee
86	Use things . . . way around.	Diana Leising
87	One friend . . . hardly possible.	Henry Adams, *The Education of Henry Adams* (1907)
87	M . . . I . . . C . . . real soon	Jimmy Dodd, *Mickey Mouse Club*
87	A shadow . . . is shining.	Benjamin Franklin
89	Su prise . . . Suuu prise	Jim Nabors, *Gomer Pyle*
89	He who laughs . . . lasts.	Terry Ferebee
91	Every once . . . has one.	Will Rogers
91	Vision is . . . the invisible	Jonathan Swift, 1711
91	Alice: ". . . you go."	Lewis Carroll, *Alice's Adventures in Wonderland*
92	For your eyes only	Ian Fleming, *For Your Eyes Only*
94	There is . . . the top.	Daniel Webster
94	The mountain top . . . empty bag.	Ted Turner
94	A celebrity is . . . being recognized.	Fred Allen, *Treadmill to Oblivion*

95	I'll take . . . hundred, Alex	*Jeopardy*
95	consistent effort . . . much prosperity	Euripides
95	The only . . . Robinson Crusoe.	Terry Ferebee
95	The slogan . . . solve problems.	Calvin Coolidge
95	Failure is no longer trying.	Elbert Hubbard
95	a lot . . . to win.	Vince Lombardi
95	Practice does . . . make perfect.	Vince Lombardi
95	The difference . . . little extra.	Terry Ferebee
95	difference between . . . exactly right	Edward Simmons
96	depends on . . . plan B	Victor Brick
96	If you . . . love Skippy	Skippy Peanut Butter, TV commercial
96	Bond, James Bond	Line from Bond movies
96	If it . . . no time.	Thomas Fuller
97	A bumper-to-bumper warranty	Lee Iacocca
97	Warp 7, Mr. Sulu	*Star Trek*

97	Nothing is . . . be overcome.	Samuel Johnson
97	A good plan . . . next week.	George Patton
97	He who . . . is last.	Mae West
98	The time to . . . is shining.	John Kennedy
98	I'd much . . . in Rome.	Caesar
99	Before you . . . to obey.	Solon, 500 B.C.
100	Better not . . . by cheating.	Sophocles
100	If A . . . mouth shut.	Einstein
102	A brand . . . $50 bill	*Bozo*
102	The Bank of Dad	Susan Bentzen-Bilkvest
102	Marry money	Walter Matthau
102	all heiresses are beautiful	King Arthur
103	Find something . . . your life.	Thomas Jefferson, 1825
104	balloon looks . . . beach ball	Gerry Faust
112	an opportunity . . . "adapt," "act."	Frank Bucaro
113	It's just . . . "the mole."	Gerry Faust
114	Speed saves . . . satisfies customers.	Tom Peters

114	What gets measured gets done.	Jay Kell
115	Steer the . . . row it.	Ann Richards
115	turn the . . . upside down.	Gerry Faust
116	you can't . . . be nice	Roger Ralph
117	If your . . . to do.	Jay Leno
117	Fewer people . . . clear accountability	Russ Cleary
118	Employees don't . . . really care.	Coleen Kolzar
119	spell out . . . to obtain	Gerry Faust
119	Can I . . . about me?	Lou Holtz
119	Kindness is . . . can hear.	Terry Ferebee
119	Those who . . . have any.	Jim Gerber
120	Spend whatever . . . and competitors.	Russ Cleary
120	long-term . . . repeat business	Tom Peters
121	Buy the . . . a risk.	Bruce McNall
121	There is . . . the hide.	Moritmar Caplan, 1963
122	"I've got . . . your help."	Larry Wilson
123	To be . . . and experience.	Glenn Wong
123	The gap . . . we do.	Frank Bucaro

123	When in . . . what's right.	Frank Uhler
124	government has . . . the parent	Alan Keyes
127	When you . . . called memoirs.	Will Rogers
127	Exit stage left	*Snagglepuss*
128	Say good night, Gracie	George Burns

ACKNOWLEDGMENTS

I sent drafts to several people whose opinion I respected. Most I knew, but some I didn't. Here is a list of those who went out of their way to review portions or all of the book and give me their ideas. You may conclude these people are generous, and they are, but please don't presume because someone's name is listed means they agree with everything I have said.

Victor Brick	Padonia Fitness Center
Bob Fitzgerald	President, HDO
Philip Gelatt	President, Northern Engraving
Joe Girard	Professional speaker
J. J. Lauderbaugh	Professional speaker
Jay Leno	Entertainer
Jay Conrad Levinson	Professional speaker
Todd Logan	Publisher
John McCarthy	Executive Director, IHRSA
Sunny Moon	Noblesville Racquet Club
Judith Neeley	Manager, Canon Club
F. G. "Buck" Rodgers	Vice President, IBM
Alan Schwartz	Chairman of the Board, TCA

Brian Swayne	F-14 navy fighter pilot
Carol Swayne	Good wife
Chuck Swayne	Professional tennis player
Frank Uhler	President, La Crosse Footwear

The following were also a big help:

Jeanne Amundson	Artist
Nickole Beckmann	University of Wisconsin
Michelle Edgar	University of Wisconsin
Florence Heintz	Marketing specialist, *La Crosse Tribune*
John P. Mann	Officer, U.S. Air Force
Joe Swayne	Helpful son